The Flourishing Advantage

A Mindset Shift from Surviving to Thriving

Dr. Wayne Hammond

WHAT PEOPLE ARE SAYING ABOUT
THE FLOURISHING ADVANTAGE

In a soft and skillful way, this is a very powerful book. It is all about connections. A flourishing life is possible, and Dr. Hammond's insights will support you on your journey. The questions after each chapter would be excellent for a study group but are also valuable as personal reflections. Too many to mention, there are many one-liners that will catch your eye, like, "People don't want to be fixed; they want to be valued," and "See people as 'at potential' not as 'at risk.'" A flourishing is derived from the Latin root for flower. As you work through the strategies presented, may you blossom into all that you were intended to be!

—John Rook, PhD
President & CEO Simon House Recovery Centre

Dr. Hammond has brilliantly combined science, experience, knowledge, and passion to inspire us to cultivate a flourishing life in ourselves and others. With newfound hope that it's never too late to start and practical personal, home, and workplace applications, the realization of untapped potential is within reach for everyone.

—Denise Blair
CEO, Calgary Youth Justice Society

At last, a book that tells the truth about how we live today—stressed, worried about our kids' futures, wracked by financial concerns, and watching from the sidelines a world that seems ready to implode. Thankfully, Dr. Wayne Hammond has taken the time to share his decades of wisdom and remedies that will shift your entire being from the depths of anxiety to one of flourishing that stems from an inner desire to create and enjoy a meaningful life. My wonderful mentor, Jim Rohn, changed my world when he said, "Work harder on yourself than you do on your job." Dr. Hammond shows you how, taking this to another level. *The Flourishing Advantage* is a must-read—make it a priority!"

—Les Hewitt
Co-Author of the #1 New York Times *bestseller* The Power of Focus
Founder of KICKON Youth Training: Empowering Marginalized Youth to Succeed in Life

If you are looking to find deeper satisfaction in your personal relationships, improve your performance at work, or just find more meaning and peace of mind in your life, *The Flourishing Advantage* has tools that will move you. Through engaging stories and practical strategies, Wayne speaks to the things that matter most in life, and his commitment to helping others jumps off the page. As a leader at home or at work, this book will provide invaluable strategies to create stronger relationships and stronger teams.

—Dr. Michael Chase
Educator, Trainer and Consultant

Here is my confession. The more stressed I am, the more stupidly I behave. Worry robs me of my best self—anxiety of my sense of equilibrium. But I've learned that what's true for me is true for all our staff, as well as the children and young people who are part of the many schools and community projects we run. That is why *The Flourishing Advantage* is a game changer. Dr. Wayne's insights and wisdom have been a huge practical help in helping us all shift from "surviving to thriving."

—Steve Chalke
Founder of Oasis Trust

As a community leader and consultant deeply rooted in First Nations perspectives, I wholeheartedly endorse this transformative book, which masterfully integrates a strengths-based approach to personal and professional development. This insightful read encourages readers to transition from merely surviving to truly thriving, offering a wealth of practical examples that resonate with our indigenous values of community and resilience. The author's approach to flourishing is not only about individual success but also about uplifting our communities as interconnected entities. This book is an essential resource for anyone looking to harness their innate strengths and foster a thriving mindset that honors and advances our collective well-being.

—Derek Bruno
Founder and CEO of SevGen Consulting, Inc.

Wayne does it again in his uniquely gracious approach of showing us the possibilities of a flourishing life. As we become aware of our thinking, habits, and negative self-talk, he gives us the tools to heal, grow, and ultimately flourish.

—*Brad Formsma*
Founder & President, I Like Giving

Dr. Hammond's lifetime of research and experience is the foundation of his practical framework for promoting individual growth, success, and impact. I know it works because I have seen his Flourishing Life Model inspire life-impacting changes in my university business students. Dr. Hammond's approach reinforces the important role of educators and business leaders who take a strengths-based approach to developing students or teams. He challenges readers to ask themselves: Am I willing to courageously take smart risks and learn from each experience so that I can flourish, and then in turn inspire my students or team to flourish?

—*Murray MacTavish, Ph.D.,*
Associate Dean, School of Business, Ambrose University

In his book, *The Flourishing Advantage*, Dr. Wayne joins the ranks of outstanding authors who have had the courage, and shown the authenticity, to find solutions and answers in some very difficult places. Pulling from decades of research and practice with a lens towards flourishing, Wayne has gifted all of us with 12 incredible chapters that kept me riveted on every page. Wayne helps us understand that when we have enough confidence to lean on our evolving strengths, we can try new things without the terror of being seen as a failure if it doesn't work out. I especially loved the chapter on Unleashing Your Potential, which helps transform your life and career with a different mindset and approach! From mindset to limiting beliefs, connecting, inspiring, building, and empowering, Wayne's passion for helping others is evident, and you will enjoy his energy, expertise, and practical approach to some common challenges.

—*Abe Brown, MBA, M.R.Ed/C, PCC*
Founder & CEO, Certified Flourishing Coaching

Copyright © 2024 by Dr. Wayne Hammond

Published by AVAIL

All rights reserved. No portion of this book may be reproduced, stored in a retrieval system, or transmitted in any form or by any means—electronic, mechanical, photocopy, recording, scanning, or other—except for brief quotations in critical reviews or articles, without prior written permission of the author.

For foreign and subsidiary rights, contact the author.

Cover design by Sara Young
Cover photo by ARGUS PHOTOGRAPHER
Author photo on cover Andrew van Tilborgh

ISBN: 978-1-962401-92-0   1 2 3 4 5 6 7 8 9 10

Printed in the United States of America

Acknowledgments

This book is not just a product of my own efforts but a testament to the incredible support system surrounding me. First and foremost, I extend my deepest gratitude to my wife, Rita, whose love and encouragement have been my anchor. To my sons, Jarod and Aaron, thank you for your endless patience and for being the joy of my daily life. Your presence has greatly enriched my understanding of flourishing.

I am also profoundly thankful to my close friend and business partner, Jeff Williams. Jeff, your unwavering support and belief in my potential have been instrumental in shaping not only this book but also my personal and professional life. You have been a pillar of strength and an endless source of inspiration.

Special thanks to Pat Springle, whose expertise in articulating complex ideas into engaging narratives has immensely enhanced this manuscript.

To all my family and friends who have been part of my journey and have contributed to the development of the ideas expressed in this book, thank you. Your influence on my life has been immeasurable, and this work would not have been possible without you.

Foreword

In *The Flourishing Advantage*, Dr. Wayne Hammond masterfully navigates the transformative journey from surviving to thriving. His profound insights into the power of leveraging personal strengths and resilience offer a refreshing and empowering perspective on personal growth. Through compelling narratives and practical applications, Dr. Hammond challenges conventional wisdom, urging readers to focus not on strengthening their weaknesses but on nurturing their inherent abilities.

This book is not just a manual for personal improvement but a call to action to embrace a life of meaning and fulfillment. Dr. Hammond's expertise and compassionate approach make this a must-read for anyone looking to enhance their capacity to flourish in an often-tumultuous world. It inspires, educates, and, most importantly, empowers readers to unlock their potential and make a lasting impact on their lives and the lives of others.

—Martijn van Tilborgh
Author, Speaker, and Entrepreneur

Contents

Introduction *13*

CHAPTER 1. **Inside Out** 15

CHAPTER 2. **Beyond Resilience** 37

CHAPTER 3. **Three Pillars**. 59

CHAPTER 4. **All in Your Head** 77

CHAPTER 5. **Connect**. 97

CHAPTER 6. **Inspire** 109

CHAPTER 7. **Build**. 125

CHAPTER 8. **Empower** 143

CHAPTER 9. **The Journey**. .157

CHAPTER 10. **Flourishing at Home** 173

CHAPTER 11. **Flourishing at Work** 193

CHAPTER 12. **Unleash Your Potential!**. 207

Appendix *217*

Introduction

When we focus on our strengths and ability to succeed—instead of mitigating or managing our weakness—we empower our capacity to thrive.
—Wayne Hammond, PhD

In the whirlwind of a fast-changing and chaotic world, the traditional approach of problem-solving has long been the go-to strategy for tackling challenges. However, our era of unprecedented uncertainty and complexity calls for a new perspective. Rather than solely focusing on remedying weaknesses or addressing problems as they arise, there is a growing recognition of the transformative power in nurturing and leveraging one's innate personal strengths to successfully navigate challenges and growth opportunities in meaningful ways. Embracing this shift involves a deliberate emphasis on *what's right* within individuals—their unique talents, strengths, and intrinsic qualities—rather than fixating on *what's wrong* or *lacking*. By shifting the spotlight toward their inherent capabilities, people are better equipped to thrive in the face of adversity and empowered to unlock their fullest potential . . . so they flourish in all aspects of life.

This paradigm shift of prioritizing innate strengths and soft skills is more than just a novel approach; it's a profound realization of the untapped reservoir of potential within each individual. By stepping out of the confines of traditional problem-solving methodologies, people embark on a journey of self-discovery and growth, embracing the courage to explore new territories and challenge their comfort zones. This courageous exploration not only fosters personal development but also opens doors to new insights, innovative solutions, and boundless opportunities. Ultimately, by embracing and nurturing their personal strengths, relational supports, and performance soft skills, people navigate life's challenges with greater ease and forge a path toward a more fulfilling and flourishing existence, characterized by authenticity, resilience, confidence, and continuous self-actualization.

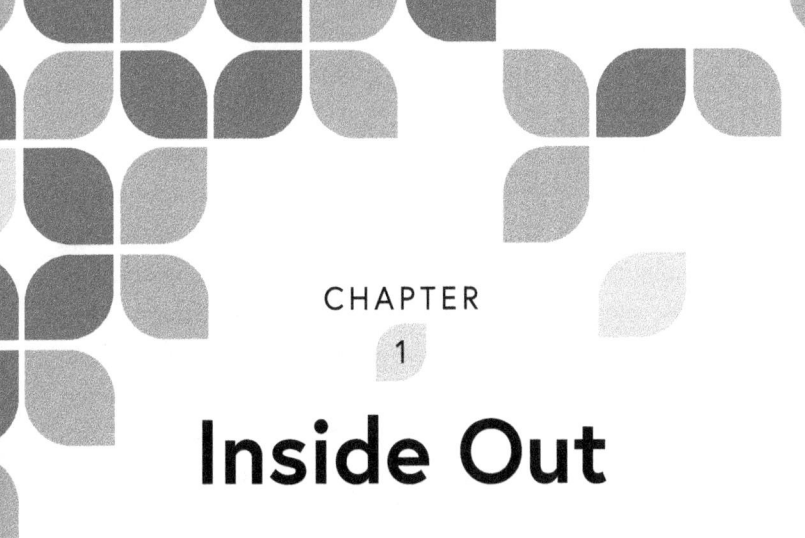

CHAPTER 1

Inside Out

Life's challenges are not supposed to paralyze you; they're supposed to help you discover who you are.
—Bernice J. Reagan

No one likes to be told they're wrong... flawed... deficient. Being exposed as "less than" certainly motivates us, but not to be open and creative. Most of us become defiant and defensive, some wither under a cloud of shame, and some just want to change the subject. Yes, we are sometimes wrong, flawed, and deficient, but are these the qualities that define us? They don't have to be. We can put on a different pair of glasses so we look at ourselves, others, and our circumstances from a far more constructive perspective. With a foundation of confidence and hope, we can handle virtually anything.

Two things are true of every person on the planet: We want our lives to have meaning, but we're afraid we don't have what it takes. This tension is at the heart of the human struggle. From our point of view, everything we do makes sense, at least at that moment. It has a purpose—to protect us from harm or advance our ambitions—even if our choices create more harm than good. We live under a set of expectations, some self-generated but many imposed by others. Success is often defined by the people around us, and we try desperately to live up to their vision of what will make us worthwhile. We may pursue a title like doctor, attorney, or teacher to give us meaning. We may strive to reach a level of power and prestige that comes with having enough money (or at least, more than "those people"). Or we measure our worth by being smarter than, more handsome or pretty than, more wealthy than, more artistic than, or a dozen other "more than" comparisons. It's no wonder most of us live this way; it's the fabric of our lived experience and the cultural air we breathe all day every day.

There's certainly nothing wrong with professional excellence, wealth, prestige, comfort, intelligence, and beauty . . . as long as they are secondary and not primary. When they're the most important way we define ourselves and our success, they satisfy only for a moment, and eventually, we realize they're not enough. . . . and we're not enough. Let me quote a few authorities on this subject, people whose conclusions might surprise you:

Few people have experienced the level of fame and fortune as Madonna. For decades, she has been an icon in our culture. Her music (and her often outlandish clothes) has garnered attention and acclaim, but in an article in *Vanity Fair,* she explained the compelling motivation that drives her:

And all of my will has always been to conquer some horrible feeling of inadequacy. I'm always struggling with that fear. I push past one spell of it and discover myself as a special human being and then I get to another stage and think I'm mediocre and uninteresting. And I find a way to get myself out of that. Again and again. My drive in life is from this horrible fear of being mediocre. And that's always pushing me, pushing me.[1]

Millions of kids play sports and have a hero they emulate—Ronaldo, LeBron James, Sue Bird, Ronald Acuña Jr., Patrick Mahomes, and more hometown stars. Over the past couple of decades, perhaps no professional athlete has eclipsed the fame of NFL quarterback Tom Brady, widely recognized as the GOAT, the greatest of all time. He led his teams to seven Super Bowl victories and was named the game's Most Valuable Player five times. After one of these victories when he was at the pinnacle of success, he remarked,

Why do I have three Super Bowl rings, and still think there's something greater out there for me? I mean, maybe a lot of people would say, "Hey man, this is what is." I reached my goal, my dream, my life. Me,

---

[1] Lynn Hirschberg, "The Misfit," *Vanity Fair,* April 1991, https://archive.vanityfair.com/article/share/bd86a835-b84c-47a7-bbec-60b9af6ea282.

> *I think: God, it's gotta be more than this. I mean this can't be what it's all cracked up to be.*[2]

Even the greatest success on the outside couldn't fill Brady's gaping hole on the inside.

In a Kenyon College commencement address, novelist David Foster Wallace looked deep into the heart of humanity and warned the graduates and their families:

> *If you worship money and things—if they are where you tap real meaning in life—then you will never have enough. Never feel you have enough. It's the truth. Worship your own body and beauty and sexual allure and you will always feel ugly, and when time and age start showing, you will die a million deaths before they finally plant you. On one level, we all know this stuff already—it's been codified as myths, proverbs, clichés, bromides, epigrams, parables: the skeleton of every great story. The trick is keeping the truth up front in daily consciousness. Worship power—you will feel weak and afraid, and you will need ever more power over others to keep the fear at bay. Worship your intellect, being seen as smart—you will end up feeling stupid, a fraud, always on the verge of being found out.*[3]

---

[2] Tom Brady, interview by Steve Kroft, *60 Minutes*, CBS, November 2005.

[3] David Foster Wallace, "Plan old untrendy troubles and emotions," *The Guardian*, 19 Sept. 2008, www.theguardian.com/books/2008/sep/20/fiction.

The outside-in approach to success promises the moon, but it can't deliver because it doesn't focus on our most fundamental human needs. Society tells us that we need to work harder to achieve a level of success that defines us as worthy. This produces enormous pressure to perform, so we live with the spoken or implied demands, "You'd better . . . ," "Good enough never is," "You mess up all the time," and the result: we learn to live with the nagging self-doubt: "What's wrong with me?" Research shows that Madonna, Tom Brady, and David Foster Wallace have it right. Even when people meet externally imposed goals, two things happen to them: they often stop striving and growing, and they feel empty and lose motivation. An article in *Forbes* quotes research about the limitations of external goals:

> *"We argue that the beneficial effects of goal setting have been overstated and that systematic harm caused by goal setting has been largely ignored," the researchers conclude. Bad "side effects" produced by goal-setting programs include a rise in unethical behavior, over-focus on one area while neglecting other parts of the business, distorted risk preferences, corrosion of organizational culture, and reduced intrinsic motivation.[4]*

So is setting goals wrong? Certainly not, but we need to ask a different set of questions: Is it possible to be highly motivated

---

[4] Sean Silverthorne, "Why Setting Goals Can Do More Harm Than Good," *Forbes*, 2 Jan. 2013, https://www.forbes.com/sites/hbsworkingknowledge/2013/01/02/why-setting-goals-can-do-more-harm-than-good/?sh=77b0cee3115a.

but from the inside out rather than chasing the criteria for success defined by society? Is it possible to construct our sense of meaning and value so that our motivation and sense of purpose don't ebb and flow with each snub and accolade, each failure and success? Can we find an internal spark that brings out the very best in us no matter the circumstances? The answer to all these questions is a resounding, "Yes!" That's what this book is about. I call it "flourishing."

Flourishing is a state of well-being characterized by a set of psychological and emotional resources that enable one to navigate life's ups and downs with a deep sense of confidence. It is marked by an inspired sense of what the future might hold, fostering optimism and resilience. Flourishing individuals are willing to scaffold their competence by venturing out of their comfort zones to explore new possibilities and embracing challenges as opportunities for growth. Additionally, they develop a strong sense of purpose and empowerment, which serves as a road map, allowing them to thrive constructively in ongoing and diverse situations.

People who flourish have that inner spark; they get excited about making a difference. They have enough confidence to lean on their evolving strengths so they can try something new without the terror of being seen as a failure if it doesn't work out. They experience an ever-deepening sense of meaning as they put themselves in a continual learning mode and regularly experience the joy of discovery.

> I had a revelation that people who came to me didn't come because they wanted to be fixed; they wanted to be valued.

This can be true for all of us. We can discover new insights about ourselves, our most important relationships, and our work, and we're able to apply what we learn in creative ways. Flourishing is never stagnant; it's about exploring, reaching, and stretching forward. After each step, we reflect so we learn just as much (or more) from setbacks as we do from successes. To live this way, we develop a deep reservoir of self-regard—not arrogance, in fact, just the opposite: We increasingly live with a beautiful blend of humility, grace, courage, and boldness because we're secure enough to know what we don't know, yet we're willing to step out of our comfort zones and try new things. People who flourish reflect a thriving mindset that embraces their innate potential and yet are patient and gracious with others because they're learning to be patient and gracious with themselves. They embrace opportunities to explore *what might be* as a way of growing their potential.

I entered training to be a psychologist because I was (and still am) fascinated by human nature, but in my training, I was taught that it was up to me to fix broken people. If I did my job well, people would no longer be anxious or depressed, their relationships would be full of love and meaning, and they'd be "normal." It was a tall order! However, in the middle of my training, I had a revelation that people who came to me didn't come because they wanted to be *fixed*; they wanted to be *valued*. That was the deeper, more transformative need they rarely could articulate. If I only focused on fixing the surface problems (which were very real and debilitating), I'd miss the opportunity to address their fundamental longing for meaning and value.

The answer, I found, is always in a person's story. This caused me to shift my approach from problem-solving to active listening, drawing from each person's deep well of lived experience of joys and heartaches. I had to move out of my role as an expert whose job was to fix their problems and become a facilitator who helps people find meaning that's inherent in their own stories. I became an active listener tuning in to hear important evidence in each person's background.

Early in my shift of perspective, I realized this principle applies to me too. I've always been resistant to people telling me what to do. It's not belligerence; I resist because this kind of instruction communicates the underlying message, "Wayne, you're wrong. You're messed up, and you'd better change!" This brought out my natural defensiveness and crushed my internal motivation to change. (I don't think I'm alone in this!) I wanted to shout, "Who are you to tell me how to live? You don't know what's going on with me!"

The solution for my clients, I discovered, is always hidden in their past experiences—their lived experiences. My job, then, was to listen, ask questions, and listen again to uncover what really matters to them. My focus was no longer on *what was wrong* with them, but on *what was right*, and *what was important* to them.

A man, I'll call him Richard, who owned a large construction company, made an appointment to see me. After brief introductions, he explained, "I run a successful company, but I'm not happy. Our company has won some very lucrative contracts, and we have very good margins. In other words, I'm making plenty of money. We've also won awards for the quality of our work. But I'm losing my kids."

"Tell me about them," I inquired.

"Both of them are in their early teens. My son is in junior high, and my daughter is a freshman in high school."

"But you feel like you're losing touch with them."

"Dr. Wayne, I don't think they like me . . . at all."

"Who else is part of this story? Tell me about your relationship with your wife."

Richard's eyes widened and he leaned back in his chair. "Oh man, it's not good. She's pretty unhappy with me too."

I could have responded, "It looks like you're doing very well in your business, so let's talk about your relationships at home," but that wouldn't have gotten to the heart of the problem. I asked another question or two, and he explained, "I'm really good at what I do at work, so I'm trying to use the same skills with my wife and kids . . . but it's just not working."

As we talked, I asked him to tell me what makes him successful in his business. He told me that the hallmark of his career is fierce determination. "Nothing stops me," he said with a measure of pride. "I keep telling my wife and children that if we just try hard enough, things will get better."

"And what's the outcome?"

"We're going in the wrong direction . . . fast."

> **He saw his wife and kids as problems to be solved instead of people to be loved.**

It quickly became apparent that Richard was treating his family like employees, and not necessarily valued employees. As a business owner, he had to have all the answers. He was in control and gave commands to those reporting to him, and he expected instant and complete obedience. If they followed his orders, things went well (at least from his point of view), and if they didn't follow orders, they paid a price. He saw himself as the solution to every business problem, and he also saw himself as the solution to every family problem.

We started with the positives. I pointed out that he was a good provider, he had tremendous skills as a leader, he was a very talented communicator, and he was dedicated to finding a way to be a better husband and father. All of those were big assets. My affirmations seemed to soften his heart. As we talked, Richard realized his interactions with his wife and children were transactional instead of relational. He saw his wife and kids as problems to be solved instead of people to be loved.

I asked, "Richard, you're obviously very skilled as a leader and highly motivated to succeed at work. What would it take for you to be as highly motivated to be the person your wife and children need?"

If I'd been problem-focused, I would have pointed out all the things he was doing wrong and given him exercises to correct them. But I took a strengths-based approach, tapping into his life's story and his strengths of persistence and grit, showing him that those qualities can propel him to be more emotionally vulnerable with his family. I asked, "What would happen if instead of giving them orders you told them, 'I don't have an answer. I don't know what we should do. I need your help'?"

Gradually, Richard realized he could be just as persistent without giving quick answers to deep, long-lasting problems. He became persistent in slowing down, listening more with his heart to genuinely understand, and valuing each person's perspectives and opinions. All of this was new to him, but he was highly motivated to change. In his business, Richard took big risks to bid for jobs that were bigger than before, and now he used his risk-taking skills to get out of his relational comfort zone and be more vulnerable. With this strengths-based approach,

Richard felt validated and encouraged to change how he related to his family. If I'd used a fault-based approach, he would almost certainly have been defensive and resistant. By tapping into his strengths, he gained hope that he could begin to mend his relationships with the people he had hurt so deeply. When he walked through my door the first time, he feared his marriage was over and he had lost his children forever, but after a few weeks of persistent vulnerability and patient listening, amazing changes were happening.

Richard had thought demanding that his wife and children try harder would fix their frayed relationships, but it had made them unravel even more. Now, he shifted his expectations from getting them to follow his orders to listening, validating, and affirming them. They began to believe that he genuinely cared for them and was invested in knowing and loving them more and more. His wife and children were amazed that he listened instead of barking orders, he admitted he needed them to be honest with him about the way he came across, and he said, more than once, words they'd never heard come from his lips: "I'm sorry. I was wrong." I explained that he shouldn't expect them to believe the change was real, at least, not at first. He would need to prove over time that he really was different.

Before Richard came to see me, virtually all his mental and emotional energy was put into his business success. He made a lot of money, but it couldn't give him what he really wanted. A portion of that energy needed to shift to his family, and to his credit, he made the change. He reorganized his schedule so he could spend both quality and quantity of time with his wife, son, and daughter. For the first time in his children's lives, he turned off his phone when he was with them. He was present and far more emotionally available to his children, even if it was only sitting in the stands at their sports activities. Day by day, he was earning their respect and trust, and soon, genuine affection blossomed.

About two years after we met, Richard brought his wife to see me. To my delight, this wasn't for a counseling session. He wanted to let me know that she had become an active participant in his business. His willingness to engage with her on an emotional level had worked wonders in their relationship. He explained, "In the past when she asked questions about my work, I was defensive and thought it was none of her business, but now I see her questions as her attempts to connect with me in a deeper way." Before they left, Richard told me, "Dr. Wayne, you saved my marriage. I have my wife back, I have my children back, and I have a life for the first time. My life has more meaning than I ever dreamed possible. It's an adventure. It's fun. All of us are learning new things together. Thank you."

That's a wonderful story, but there's more: Richard presented the flourishing model he'd learned to the members of his state's construction board, and now he's training business owners and engineers in construction to reframe their lives so they can move beyond external success to experience complete flourishing. He told me, "They need more in their lives than blueprints, budgets, and bulldozers. Just like me, they need to reorient their perspective and mindset to what really matters. In my presentations, I'm moving away from lecturing at the front of the room to a coaching model so I can walk side by side with them because relationships have more impact than mere knowledge."

Let me tell another remarkable story: A state organization that works with high-risk young people asked me to consult with them. Their clients are often living on the street and addicted to a wide range of drugs. Their goal is to minimize risks for these kids—the media has a field day criticizing agencies like this when something goes tragically wrong with one of the kids, so they're always on edge. I shared with the staff members that it's important to see people, especially people like their clients, as "at potential" instead of just "at risk." When we view them through the lens of possibilities, we instill hope and courage, even if it takes a while for the message to sink in. But if we see them through the lens of liability, they intuitively sense that we don't believe in them, and we only want to control them so they don't ruin their lives on our watch. (In other words, it's more about us than them.) When youth in care reach the age of sixteen, they'll be on their own. If we haven't uncovered their strengths and empowered them to thrive, their futures usually look bleak.

At one of my presentations to the staff members, I met a case worker, I'll call her Marcia, who told me about a girl, I'll call her Bethany, who had been living on the street since she was twelve. She had been on heroin, become a prostitute, and had three abortions by the time she was sixteen. When I shared the concepts of a flourishing life, I'm sure some of the case workers rolled their eyes, but when Marcia spoke, they instantly resonated with her. She knew that trying to manage the behavior of her clients often produced resistance and rebellion. Instead, in her relationship with Bethany, she became a surrogate mother who loved her and believed in her future, in spite of outward appearances and the pattern of tragic, self-destructive past experiences.

Marcia shared that she didn't bring a checklist of requirements to demand compliance from Bethany. She started with the perspective of accepting Bethany for who she was now, not what she or others thought she should be. This approach startled the young woman who had never experienced love before. In fact, Bethany didn't know how to handle Marcia's openhanded and full-hearted regard. Later she explained that she wondered if Marcia was trying to get something from her, and her kindness was a manipulative technique. It took time for Bethany to believe it was real. I often tell social workers that when clients push back against expressions of kindness and compassion, the social workers are on the right track. The clients' response isn't opposition; it's inexperience and fear—they just want to know if the expressions of love are genuine. Organizations that work with troubled young people often explain the high dropout rate by saying, "The kids just weren't motivated." But that's not the problem. It's important to understand that our brain is designed to survive, not to thrive. The primitive part of the human brain, the amygdala, is constantly scanning the environment four to five times a second looking for a threat. For most youth in care, this protective mechanism and survival instinct is hyper-vigilant.

As a result, trust isn't their first response because of their lived experience of pain and feeling vulnerable. The starting point for positive change is based on two important factors: First, is the youth connected to a safe, trusting, and caring relationship with a caring adult? And second, is the youth supported in ways that reflect what they consider meaningful? The problem is that the caseworkers tend to ignore the client's hidden motivations. Youth don't want to mess up their lives; they just don't understand the strengths and skills that are necessary to meet their needs in successful and supported ways.

For a couple of years, I worked with Marcia's agency and had the pleasure of getting regular updates from her about Bethany, but I'd never met the young woman. At a conference, I gave a talk on the strengths-based approach to social work. When I finished, I sat at a table with other presenters. One was a young woman who was going to give her testimony. It was Bethany. As we sat at the table, I asked her to tell me her story. I was mesmerized by the depth and breadth of the change she'd experienced through her relationship with Marcia. When Bethany finished speaking, I was deeply moved. With a quivering voice, I told her, "Bethany, you are one of the most amazing people I've ever met. You have taught me so much in the last fifteen minutes—what it means to persevere, what it means to rise above tragic circumstances. I want to thank you for telling me your story."

I asked about her plans for the future. She smiled and said, "I want to be a caseworker like Marcia. I'm looking forward to my classwork."

I told her, "You'll be amazing because you have a life story that will connect—in the deepest, most meaningful way—with the people you're going to help. You'll touch the hearts of kids like very few people can."

Three years later, Bethany invited me to attend her graduation. When it was her turn to walk across the stage and receive her diploma, she stopped and pointed to me. She said, "That's Dr. Hammond. He told me I could do this, and I did it!"

I hadn't walked with Bethany during those years when Marcia loved her like a mother, but in those few minutes we shared at the conference three years before her graduation, my meager words of heartfelt affirmation meant something to her. That's the power of kindness, of affirming what we see in others by accepting them for who they are now (not for what we think they should be), believing in their potential, and taking the time to notice what's meaningful to them. As always, the solution—the hope and motivation that her life could really count—was realized by aligning her strengths with her aspirations through a relationship of unconditional support.

Today, Bethany is an incredibly effective social worker. The people she serves soak up her optimism and bold faith that life can be so much better. They believe her because they see it evidenced in her lived experience and story. She's married and has three children. Years ago, she was homeless, addicted, alone, and struggling with her sense of personal value and purpose. Now, she's inspiring her family and those she works with—whose lives are forever changed by the magnetism of her tenacious resilience and her capacity to thrive. If you want to know what it means to flourish, talk to Bethany.

Bethany isn't a one-off story. Again and again, I've seen the amazing power of strength-based support, teaching, parenting, and leading. When we connect with people so that they feel safe and become convinced that we believe in them, our words can change the trajectory of their lives. We may walk with them for decades, or it may only be a five-minute conversation, but our presence, our kindness, and our belief in them give them the confidence to step out and do the amazing things they were created to do. Brittany's story is a case study of one of the most important principles in human thriving:

- How people *feel* determines how they *think* about themselves and their potential.
- How people *think* about themselves determines their *coping* response.
- And how people *cope* in repeated situations determines their *convictions*.

Positive change is a process from the inside out. Bethany was able to feel differently about who she was, embrace a new way of thinking about possibilities, courageously step out of her comfort zone with new ways of coping, and ultimately experience a deep sense of self-confidence and empowerment. Certainly, it was her journey of remarkable growth, but it started with a deep, ongoing connection with a caring adult.

Embracing a mindset centered around personal belief and the ability to grow our potential from within is crucial for genuine thriving and self-fulfillment. When we shift our focus from external validation and societal expectations to nurturing an internal belief in our capacity for growth, we unlock a new source of resilience and empowerment. By acknowledging that our potential isn't fixed but continuously evolving, we embrace a transformative belief that propels us forward on our journey of self-discovery and self-actualization. This inside-out approach allows us to redefine success on our terms, prioritizing personal growth, authenticity, and inner fulfillment over external measures of achievement. Moreover, by viewing mistakes as valuable opportunities for learning and growth rather than reflections of our worth, we cultivate a mindset of resilience, self-compassion, and boundless potential. Ultimately, embracing this transformative belief empowers us to thrive from within, embracing our unique journey with courage, authenticity, and unwavering determination.

Our ultimate goal isn't to manufacture an easy life. The only life worth living is a flourishing one, based on the bedrock of learned wisdom and the commitment to never stop learning, stretching, and growing. Actually, we only take steps toward genuine fulfillment when we face challenges, and whether we succeed or fail in the first attempts, we learn valuable lessons for the next time. This is smart risk-taking, this is where you discover strengths you never knew were there, and this is where life becomes an adventure instead of a grind.

Flourishing isn't a solitary enterprise. It doesn't happen on our own. We are deeply relational creatures—that includes all of us, no matter what our personality profiles might say about us. Even the most introverted people can't thrive and flourish without a few close connections. We need people to cheer us on when we take courageous steps, comfort and encourage us when we fail, and partner with us as we navigate the complex matrix of life together. Choosing the right people is crucial. Some will be with us for a long time, and others for only a moment, but supportive connections are absolutely essential for us to stay on the journey of wise risk-taking, growing, and making a difference in the lives of others.

Many people are very uncomfortable with emotions like hurt, fear, sadness, anger, and anxiety, but these are normal human responses to difficult situations. People who flourish don't repress these feelings and hope they go away, and they aren't crushed under the weight of them. Instead, they use each instance of painful emotions as an opportunity to reflect and grow. Sometimes powerful emotions can overwhelm a person, and medical intervention is necessary, but in many cases, they overwhelm them because the person hasn't adequately processed them for years and the cumulative effect has caused a physiological breakdown. It's better to be honest about them as they happen and learn the lessons we need to learn. If we haven't dealt with them before, now is the time to start.

It's my personal belief that every person is of infinite value. You were created for a purpose and are shaped by your story of past and evolving experiences—not to hold you back but to become stepping stones to something magnificent. Your future is incredibly bright because you can discover hidden strengths you can use to make a difference in the world around you. Your past may have held you hostage, but no longer. People who live in the past often struggle with depression over the unresolved losses they've suffered, those who are afraid in the present are anxious about every decision and interaction, and those who are pessimistic about the future feel hopeless and angry—and some of us fall in all three categories!

In the following chapters, we'll look at the difference between resilience and flourishing, we'll explore the four components of a flourishing life, and we'll see how the principles and practices of flourishing apply to our most important relationships.

What if you got up each day with a strong hope, plenty of energy, and genuine enthusiasm?

What if your failures became springboards for growth?

What if you were no longer shackled by the fear of failure so your creativity could soar?

What if your strongest motivations came from the inside out instead of being imposed on you by circumstances or others?

What if you had relationships with a few people who know the worst about you and love you still?

What if you found the key to a truly flourishing life?

At the end of each chapter, you'll find some questions to prompt deeper reflection and stimulate discussion with others who are reading the book. This isn't a time trial, so don't rush through the questions. Take your time to consider how your story is the springboard to a flourishing future.

Think about it:

1) What are the implicit promises of success, pleasure, and approval? Why are they inadequate foundations for flourishing?
2) Who do you know who lives with inside-out motivation? What's true of that person's purpose, confidence, and relationships?
3) Take some time to write elements of your life's story on a timeline. Be as detailed as you want to be.
4) What emotions resurfaced as you recalled pleasant and painful experiences?
5) Do you believe that your story holds the key to a genuinely meaningful and flourishing life? Why or why not?
6) What do you hope to get out of this book?

CHAPTER 2

Beyond Resilience

"The only real voyage of discovery exists, not in seeing new landscapes, but in having new eyes."
—Marcel Proust

Resilience is bouncing back from adversity, but *flourishing* is bouncing forward to new opportunities. We say people are resilient when they have the tenacity to withstand and recover from painful or challenging situations. It's returning to the baseline by coping with stress and setbacks well enough so they're not derailed by the experiences. The goal is to regain stability and restore equilibrium. We can applaud, and even be amazed at, people who endure severe suffering and find their way through.

People naturally feel stressed, physically tired, and overwhelmed by the increasing challenges of life. In general, most people draw upon a level of energy required to adapt in positive ways during life-changing and stressful situations. This ability to adapt well despite adversity is referred to as the capacity to be resilient.

Resilience is a self-righting ability to bounce back and successfully adapt when faced with difficult circumstances, but the capacity to be resilient is an uneven process—a person might be resilient in one situation but need a higher level of support in a different setting. Resilience isn't invulnerability to stress or the trait of a "perfect person." Instead, it reflects a growth mindset: the courage to take smart risks to grow their potential in purposeful ways. When they take these steps, they increase their capacity to be resilient and experience profound personal growth.

Flourishing is that, but it's more than that. It shifts the focus from getting back to the baseline to advancing, thriving, and personal growth. People who flourish continuously push their baseline forward, taking the required smart risks and learning from each experience. The result is emotional authenticity (because they aren't afraid of their feelings), personal integrity (because they have nothing to hide), growth, fulfillment, and the thrill of seeing their positive impact on others. The eventual outcome of flourishing isn't just resilience but a state of optimal well-being, enhanced performance, and personal development. It taps into our deepest sense of purpose and draws out our highest potential.

Figure 1: The Influence of Flourishing

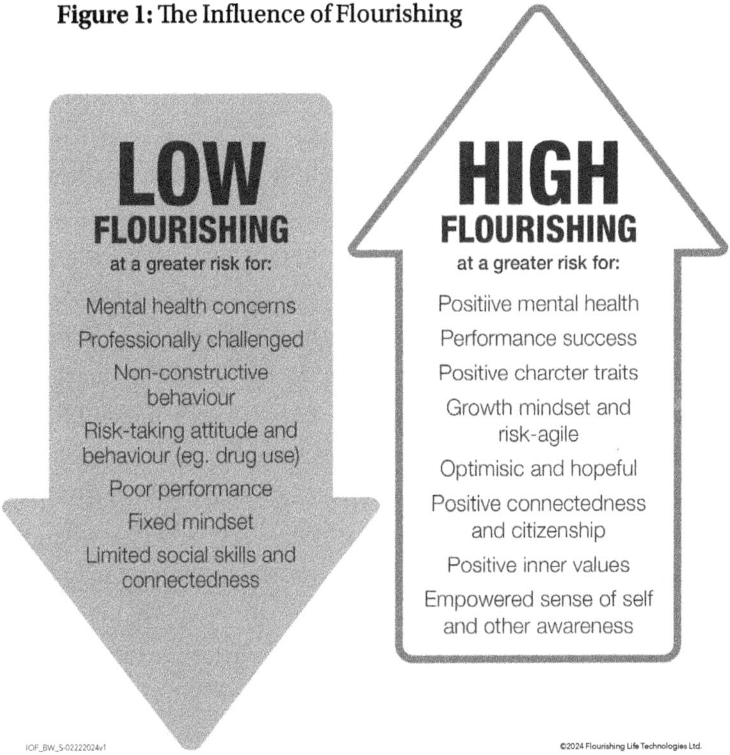

LOW FLOURISHING
at a greater risk for:

Mental health concerns
Professionally challenged
Non-constructive behaviour
Risk-taking attitude and behaviour (eg. drug use)
Poor performance
Fixed mindset
Limited social skills and connectedness

HIGH FLOURISHING
at a greater risk for:

Positiive mental health
Performance success
Positive charcter traits
Growth mindset and risk-agile
Optimisic and hopeful
Positive connectedness and citizenship
Positive inner values
Empowered sense of self and other awareness

©2024 Flourishing Life Technologies Ltd.

By purposefully developing flourishing strengths and related professional skills, you will enhance your experience of:

- Living with a sense of purpose and happiness at home and at work,
- Connectedness and rapport with others,
- Personal empowerment and confidence,

- A growing capacity for effective performance and satisfaction at work,
- Balance with your overall health and sense of positive well-being,
- Achieving your life's passions and professional goals, and
- Enjoying a sense of meaning and direction.

As a therapist, I was trained to help people deal with past hurts and bad choices, but I didn't learn how to help them go further and use their experiences to give them the wisdom to handle life's challenges more effectively in the future. Before I grasped the flourishing model, I helped people deal with one problem, then another, and then another. I was making them dependent on me, not encouraging them to be strong, wise, and independent people. This limiting pattern was especially true when I worked with addicts and people who had suffered domestic violence. When addicts went to treatment, they usually faced their flaws and admitted they had made a series of bad decisions. When abuse victims found safe havens and came for counseling, most of them made commitments to avoid abusers for the rest of their lives. But the recidivism statistics aren't encouraging: 40 to 60 percent of addicts and alcoholics relapse within a month of leaving treatment, and 85 percent relapse within a year.[5] Approximately 50 percent of domestic abuse victims return to the original abuser or find someone else who treats them the same way. Among the array of reasons are:

---

[5] Family Addiction Specialist, "10 Most Common Reasons for Addiction Relapse," https://www.familyaddictionspecialist.com/blog/10-most-common-reasons-for-addiction-relapse.

- The fear that the abuser's actions will become more violent and may become lethal if the victim attempts to leave.
- Unsupportive friends and family.
- Knowledge of the difficulties of single parenting and reduced financial circumstances.
- The victim feeling that the relationship is a mix of good times, love, and hope along with manipulation, intimidation, and fear.
- The victim's lack of knowledge of or access to safety and support.
- Fear of losing custody of any children if they leave or divorce their abuser or fear the abuser will hurt, or even kill, their children."[6]

I was making them dependent on me, not encouraging them to be strong, wise, and independent people.

Those who return to their addiction or an abuser may have experienced some distance from their triggers in treatment or a safe place, but only for a while. If they don't internalize crucial

---

6 "Why Do Victims Stay?" *National Coalition Against Domestic Violence (NCADV)*, https://ncadv.org/why-do-victims-stay.

lessons that propel them forward into new ways of thinking, acting, and relating, it's easy to slip back into familiar, destructive patterns. In other words, it's not enough to stop drinking or using, and it's not enough to get away from an abuser. Real emotional, psychological, and relational health takes more; it takes the tools of flourishing. When people uncover their innate strengths and put them into practice, a new world opens up to them. They're less and less dependent on a system to protect them, and they're increasingly empowered to thrive. They then say, "I wouldn't have chosen the pain I've endured (and inflicted on others), but I've learned from it. I know how to create success that reinforces my sense of value and purpose." The old saying might be trite, but it's true: "What do you do with a bunch of lemons? You make lemonade."

I work with several school systems that serve the indigenous community in our area, and I teach a class called "How to Fail." Many of the students come from families that have been marginalized for generations. Addictions and abuse are common, along with the natural results: hopelessness, seething anger, and shame. So why in the world would I teach a class on failure? Because I want to encourage them to stretch their creative wings and launch into the air. If they fall, I want them to know that's not the end of the world. In fact, it's the beginning of something wonderful! I ask them to work together with a team of other students so they learn the art of collaboration and discover the power of affirmation. For me, it's a lot of fun to watch them come up with novel ideas and solutions. I point out what I see: "When you did that, you were persevering." "When you kept asking questions, you demonstrated a growth mindset." "When you helped others on your team accomplish their task, you were a team player." I try to identify a positive action by each student. Their experience and my affirmation don't just feel good; they actually change the neural wiring in their brains. A success created out of a courageous, creative risk writes a new pathway in the brain, one that will stimulate and reinforce each new creative pursuit (more on this later).

The concept of flourishing isn't just textbook theory to me. I've lived it. When I was in the third grade, my teacher became frustrated with my lack of progress and pronounced, "Wayne, you're stupid!" It was a label that stuck, branded deep in my soul. For almost twenty years, I believed I was mentally deficient because I couldn't learn like the other kids. I was convinced I'd never read or write. When I was twenty-seven, I decided to give college a try. My first attempt at writing a paper as part of the application didn't go well. On an entrance exam, I scored 10 out of 100. Thankfully, I met a professor who changed my life. He told me, "Wayne, you have some good ideas, but you don't know how to express them. I'll teach you how to read, write, and study so you can succeed in college." He worked with me for eight months, patiently drawing out my latent strengths and teaching me how to study. When I applied again, I met the criteria to be accepted, even though I was much older than the other incoming freshmen. When I got the grade back from my first paper, it said A+. I made a 4.0 that semester . . . and excelled academically every semester for the next fifteen years of college, graduate school, and doctoral work.

What happened? What turned my life around? It was when one person saw strengths in me that no one else saw, believed in me, and walked with me as I took halting steps of progress. Each success gave me more confidence that I could reach a little higher and succeed a little more.

> I could have chosen to remain in the bubble, but instead, I took a chance to see if what he saw in me could become a new normal for my life.

All people want to be successful, and they all want their lives to be full of meaning, but they don't know how to get there. Their lived experiences have communicated a powerful, negative message that they've accepted and believed with all their hearts. In response, they try desperately to win approval, but they live in fear of being ignored or ridiculed; they're determined to never feel inferior or vulnerable again, so they act out in ways to protect themselves; or they've given up on purpose, meaning, and connections, so they drift in self-contained bubbles, hoping no one will see inside and notice their anxiety. I had been one of those in the bubble of isolation and despair, but the professor identified my strengths, imparted the skills, and believed in me so I could flourish. At that point, it was up to me to take advantage of the wealth of opportunities he had given me. I could have chosen to remain in the bubble, but instead, I took a chance to see if what he saw in me could become a new normal for my life.

Is anyone too far gone to enjoy a flourishing life? I don't think so. At least, I've never met anyone like that. As I write this chapter, I'm reminded of a man I met just a few weeks ago. He had been a member of Hell's Angels for thirty years, fifteen of which he'd spent in prison for violent offenses. He related, "When I was in prison, a lady came to help some of us get our GEDs. Several of us, like me, were in their forties and fifties, not exactly on the cusp of getting a job for the first time. This was the first time someone showed genuine interest in me as a person. She talked to me about my goals and dreams, and she seemed genuinely interested in who I was and my aspirations. For thirty years, the jacket I wore and the bike I rode caused people to stereotype me, but she saw beneath all that." Her influence brought out something in him that he didn't even know was there. When he got out of prison, he wanted to help kids on the street avoid the pain, rage, and emptiness he'd felt. He opened a shop to repair and refurbish motorcycles, and he invited kids from the neighborhood to join him. He told me, "I grab sixteen kids, and together, we rebuild a bike. It may take us two months, but I'm not in a hurry. It's all about the relationships I build with them. With a wrench in our hands and grease on our faces, I ask, 'Hey, what do you want to do with your life?' We have incredible conversations."

This tough guy had been hiding a tender heart for decades. When a lady stepped into his world in prison and saw something wonderful in him, the trajectory of his life radically changed. Before, his life's story was about an outcast, someone no one should mess with, but she refused to see him that way.

ELEMENTS OF FLOURISHING

Let me unpack more about flourishing: The capacity to flourish, from a strengths-based perspective, refers to an individual's inherent ability to thrive and reach their full potential. It focuses on identifying and nurturing a person's unique strengths, talents, and resources rather than focusing primarily on deficits or weaknesses. In every kind of relationship—marriage, parenting, teaching, leading, work, and even friendships—this perspective radically changes interactions and outcomes. In most cases, well-intentioned people have pointed out problems, failures, vulnerabilities, and deficits in attempts to help the other person change, but far too often, this emphasis discourages rather than inspires. Focusing on "what's right" as the starting point for positive change, success, and sustainable well-being is far more productive (though it requires significant effort to make this crucial shift in focus). Flourishing facilitates success in various domains of life and produces a sense of well-being, fulfillment, and resilience in the face of challenges. It leverages strengths to overcome obstacles, build meaningful connections, and lead a purposeful and satisfying life.

Some key characteristics of those who flourish include:

Positive emotions: People who flourish experience frequent positive emotions such as joy, gratitude, and optimism, even in the face of challenges. When faced with pleasant situations, they savor the positive experiences and use these emotions as a source of motivation and resilience. In challenging situations, their positive emotions can serve as a buffer against stress and help maintain a positive outlook.

Meaning and purpose: Flourishing is characterized by a deep, abiding sense of meaning and purpose, giving individuals a reason to thrive and contributing to their well-being and resilience in both positive and challenging contexts.

Engagement: When people live with a strong sense of purpose, they become deeply engaged in activities to fulfill that purpose. They experience "a state of flow" where they're fully focused on the task at hand. People who flourish demonstrate an enhanced capacity to engage life's challenges in competent ways. They are perpetual learners, acquiring knowledge and skills they can use in new situations.

Positive relationships: People who flourish have strong and supportive social networks. These relationships provide a source of emotional support and assistance during challenging times. Additionally, they can enhance the enjoyment of positive situations by sharing experiences with loved ones.

Adaptability: When circumstances change, whether for better or worse, people who are flourishing tend to adjust more readily and make the most of the new situation. They're open to learning and growth, even in uncertain or unfamiliar environments.

Accomplishment and achievement: They set and pursue meaningful goals, experiencing a sense of accomplishment and satisfaction when they achieve their objectives.

Growth-focused: They embrace the importance of learning, so they often discover new strengths by learning from mistakes and stepping out of their comfort zone with courage, curiosity, and self-empowerment.

Resilience: Flourishing is associated with higher levels of resilience, which means individuals can bounce back from adversity more effectively. When confronted with challenges, they draw upon their cultivated psychological well-being and emotional stability to cope and adapt. They view setbacks as opportunities for growth rather than insurmountable obstacles or inescapable labels that scream: "Failure!"

Self-acceptance: They have a positive self-image and accept themselves for who they are, embracing their strengths and weaknesses with self-compassion.

Autonomy: They have a sense of autonomy and agency, moving forward with confidence. Flourishing includes the belief in one's ability to achieve goals and overcome obstacles. This self-belief empowers people to take constructive actions in both positive and adverse situations. They are more likely to persevere and effectively problem-solve.

Physical health: They prioritize their physical health and well-being, engaging in activities that promote physical vitality.

Psychological well-being: They experience a high level of psychological well-being, characterized by a sense of inner peace, contentment, and fulfillment. Those who flourish tend to be optimistic about the future, but it's not blind hope. This optimism enables them to approach both good and challenging situations with a sense of hope and confidence. They are more likely to set and work towards meaningful goals, even when facing difficulties.

Overall, a flourishing person embodies a holistic sense of well-being, thriving across multiple domains of life with a deep sense of fulfillment and purpose.

How can we experience these benefits? Only if we undergo a significant paradigm shift in our thinking, beliefs, and behavior.

THE PARADIGM SHIFT

The concept of flourishing represents a significant paradigm shift in the fields of psychology, well-being, and personal development. Traditionally, much of psychological research and practice had been focused on identifying and addressing what's wrong with individuals (such as mental illnesses, negative behavioral coping strategies, or emotional deficits). However, the flourishing paradigm shifts the focus from what's wrong to what's right with individuals and communities. Here's how this shift unfolds:

Positive psychology: Flourishing is closely associated with positive psychology, a relatively new branch of psychology that emerged in the late 20th century. Positive psychology emphasizes the study of strengths, virtues, and factors that contribute to a fulfilling and meaningful life. It investigates what makes life worth living, rather than just diagnosing and treating psychological disorders.

Emphasis on well-being: Flourishing places a central emphasis on well-being, encompassing not only the absence of illness but also the presence of positive qualities and experiences. It considers emotional, psychological, and social well-being, all of which contribute to an individual's overall thriving.

A strengths-based approach: One of the key aspects of the flourishing paradigm is the adoption of a strengths-based approach. Instead of focusing primarily on weaknesses and deficits, it encourages identifying and nurturing an individual's or community's strengths, talents, and resources.

Cultivating positive traits: The flourishing paradigm identifies and encourages positive traits such as gratitude, resilience, optimism, and empathy. These qualities are seen as fundamental building blocks of a flourishing life.

The goal of personal growth: Flourishing recognizes that personal growth and self-actualization are ongoing processes. It encourages individuals to set and pursue meaningful goals, develop a sense of purpose, and continuously strive for self-improvement and fulfillment.

A shift toward prevention and promotion: While traditional psychology often focuses on treating mental health issues once they arise, the flourishing paradigm promotes prevention and proactive well-being. It equips individuals and communities with the tools needed to flourish and thrive before problems become severe.

A holistic perspective: Flourishing takes a holistic view of human well-being, acknowledging the fact that it involves multiple dimensions, including physical, mental, emotional, and social aspects. It recognizes the interconnectedness of these dimensions in promoting a flourishing life.

Community and societal implications: Beyond individual well-being, the flourishing paradigm has implications for building more positive and resilient communities and societies. It underscores the importance of social connections, community support, and policies that promote well-being at a broader level.

In essence, flourishing represents a shift in focus from a deficit-based model to a strengths-based, positive, and holistic model of well-being. It acknowledges that individuals and communities have the capacity not only to overcome challenges but also to thrive, grow, and lead fulfilling lives by nurturing their inherent strengths and positive qualities—and everyone has them! This paradigm shift has had a profound impact on psychology, counseling, leadership, education, and various other fields because it provides a more balanced and comprehensive approach to enhancing human potential and well-being.

At the most basic and immediate level, many of us see our emotions as a threat to our safety and security. Painful ones, like hurt, fear, anger, sadness, and shame, are, indeed, "flashing lights on the dashboard of our hearts." But what do we do when we're driving along and we see the light flash, indicating our car is overheating, a tire is low, or we're running out of gas? If we ignore the lights, we'll almost certainly experience far greater trouble a few miles down the road. But panic isn't a good option either. When our anxiety eclipses our ability to think, we make bad decisions and compound the problem. How then, can our emotions help us move forward? The message of our emotions is to pay attention and enlist the strengths we either already possess or that we're developing.

FUNDAMENTAL PRINCIPLES

It's often helpful to get a snapshot of the principles inherent in any model, whether in engineering a bridge or building a flourishing life. Look at these traits of people who focus on their strengths instead of their deficiencies:

- Those who flourish are aware of their unique strengths and competencies.
- Their strengths, not their weaknesses and flaws, are the foundation of their identities.
- The more they maximize their strengths, the more their strengths become powerful and effective.
- All of us are doing the best we can with what we've experienced and how we've learned to cope up to this point. Our coping strategies make perfect sense to us.
- When they feel secure and valued, all people, regardless of personality or background, want to explore opportunities and contribute in constructive ways. It's in our DNA.

- A person's capacity to thrive can be realized when he or she is supported with the right conditions and resources.
- Focusing on obstacles and flaws limits our creativity to find new solutions to old problems.
- People who feel valued are receptive to inspiring ideas.
- Flourishing is never stagnant; it's either growing or ebbing.
- Positive change happens in the context of safe, unconditional, and authentic relationships.
- Self-regard is more important than what others think about us.

Some who read these principles think, *So what's new? That's the way I've been living.* But many have a different reaction: *I can't imagine living this way! Sign me up!*

THE FOUR PHASES OF TRANSFORMATIONAL CHANGE

Change from the outside-in seldom lasts, but inside-out transformation becomes a lifestyle. I don't believe people change simply by acquiring information. Instead, genuine transformation happens when people experience four strategic phases of strengths-based change: Connect, Inspire, Build, and Empower (CIBE; see Figure 2). These phases need to be experienced sequentially and purposefully to create the emotional connection, foundational belief, and progressive-experiential learning for positive and sustainable change. This process transforms people from the *inside out* (facilitating a positive belief, supported by positive relational influences, prepared with insightful skills/knowledge, and empowered competence through a scaffolding and stretching journey of thriving) as opposed to the traditional strategy of an *outside-in* approach (managing change through delivery of prescribed behavioral interventions and imparted knowledge).

Much of the rest of this book is about the process required to craft a flourishing life. The four components are:

1) Connect

As we've seen, we're created as relational creatures, and we function well only when we feel safe and valued in stable relationships. Without these connections, we're left with an array of coping strategies to please people to win their approval, strive to prove we're valuable, dominate others so they can't hurt us, or hide physically or emotionally so no one can get too close. But with powerfully affirming human connections, we feel free to explore and take risks without the fear of ridicule.

2) Inspire

In this stage, we're invited to reframe our stories, from anxious to confident, from desperate to calm and reasoned, and from fearful to bold. We're more understanding and patient with those who struggle with life's heartaches because we realize all of us are simply doing the best we can in light of the circumstances of our pasts. But in a relationship of security, safety, encouragement, and unconditional regard, we're inspired to reach for new goals.

3) Build

As we're inspired to take new risks, we learn from our failures as well as our successes (and if we're secure enough, we learn more from our failures than our successes). In this stage, we develop latent skills and acquire new ones, we gain wisdom in how to maximize our strengths, and our goals become clarified as we grow more confident.

In this stage, we also develop our soft skills, the ability to relate to others in productive ways. Hard skills can be taught in a classroom and fine-tuned in experience, but soft skills are honed in the give and take of relating to people in various situations. Hard skills often open doors of opportunity, but soft skills enable us to be excellent team members and team leaders . . . and get promoted.

4) Empower

The goal of those of us who are parents, teachers, executives, coaches, and team leaders isn't to use people to fulfill our aims but to empower them to be all they can be, which always produces wins for everyone. People in this stage are autonomous learners, continually stretching and growing, and enjoying a network of creative partners.

56 THE FLOURISHING ADVANTAGE

We can conceptualize the phases like this:

Figure 2: CIBE - The Four Phases of Transformation Change

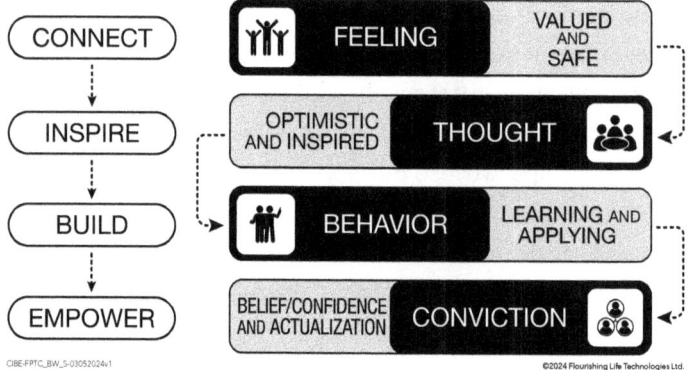

This is the pathway to a flourishing life, but before we explore these phases, we'll take a longer look at the importance of changing our mindsets—the way we see ourselves, others, challenges, and opportunities.

Think about it:

1) What are some similarities and differences between resilience and flourishing?
2) What are some reasons why getting back to baseline seems good enough? Why isn't it?
3) How might you have responded if you were a student and a new teacher taught your class "How to Fail"?
4) Look back at the elements of flourishing. Which ones are most attractive to you? Explain your answer.

5) How would you describe the paradigm shift from focusing on what's wrong with us to focusing on what's right with us? What difference would this shift make (or does it already make) in your life?
6) How would you rate the quality of your connection with at least one person who believes in you? How much do you feel free to be inspired to do something creative and new? How well are you building a reservoir of knowledge and skills? How much do you feel empowered to be all you can be?

CHAPTER

Three Pillars

In my years of working with people, I've seen a clear pattern in the lives of those who flourish. They grow if and when certain strength factors are in place: Pillar One: Personal strengths, Pillar Two: Environmental strengths, and Pillar Three: Performance strengths. As shown in Figure 3a these three pillars overlap and interlock, reinforcing one another.

Figure 3a: The **Flourishing Life** Model™

PERSONAL STRENGTHS	ENVIRONMENTAL STRENGTHS	PERFORMANCE STRENGTHS
Self-Awareness	Home Life Influence	Internal Soft Skills/Traits
Social-Awareness	Work/Role Influence	External Soft Skills/Traits
Self-Management	Peer Influence	Mastery Skills/Traits
Self-Care	Learning Influence	
	Community Influence	

Figure 3b: The Flourishing Life Strengths Framework
(see Appendix for Strength Definitions)

PILLAR ONE

PERSONAL STRENGTHS
(Personal Perception and Inner Strengths)

Self-Awareness
- Self-Esteem/Optimistic
- SB Perspective/Confidence
- Sense of Purpose/Direction

Social-Awareness
- Empathic/Caring
- Positive Social Skills
- Social Conscience/Altuistic

Self-Management
- Emotional Awareness/Self-Regulation
- Self-Efficacy/Empowered
- Cognitive Flexibility/Adaptable

Self-Care
- Self-Kindness/Compassion
- Spiritual Eagerness
- Health Aware/Active

PILLAR TWO

ENVIRONMENTAL STRENGTHS
(Environmental Influence and Support Strengths)

Home Life Influence/Support
- Connectedness – Valued/Safe/Belonging
- Positive Expectations/Support
- Positive Communication/Respect

Work/Role/Support
- Connectedness – Valued/Safe/Belonging
- Positive Expectations/Support
- Positive Communication/Respect

Peer Influence/Support
- Positive Friends/Acceptance
- Shared Values/Peer Refusal

Learning Influence/Support
- Achievement Motivated
- Competence Focused
- Confidence Building

Community Influence/Support
- Connectedness – Valued/Safe/Belonging
- Positive Expectations/Support
- Positive Communication/Involvement

PILLAR THREE

PERFORMANCE STRENGTHS
(Performance Skills and Character Strengths)

Internal Soft Skills/Traits
- Perserverance/Grit
- Managing Stress/Mindfulness
- Perceptiveness/Prudence
- Growth Mindset
- Criticism/Change Receptive
- Integrity/Ethical/Courage

External Soft Skills/Traits
- Communication/Listening
- Empowering/Generous
- Positive Interpersonal Skills
- Diverse/Cultural Receptive
- Managing Conflict/Expectations
- Positive Influence/Team Player

Mastery Hard Skills/Traits
- Innovative/Creative
- Knowledgeable/Intuitive
- Critical Thinker/Problem Solver
- Good Judgment/Accountable
- Curious/Inquiry Skills
- Continuous/Deep Learner

More specifically, the ability to flourish is dependent on two critical concepts—the capacity to be resilient and to competently draw upon critical performance soft skills (See Figure 4). The capacity for resilience is a result of how a person develops their self-awareness and inner strengths as they interact with their environmental influences and relational supports such as work/school, family, peers, and community. One's performance skills and character traits develop through active-experiential learning opportunities that nurture one's understanding and capacity to draw upon the critical performance soft skills and character traits required to perform in successful ways.

Figure 4: The Two Critical Components of Flourishing

The Role of Resilience and Competence

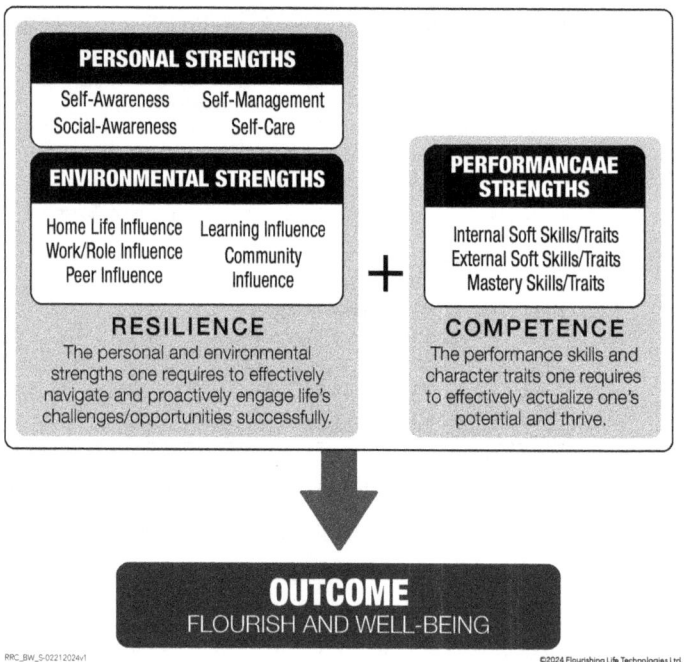

THE FIRST PILLAR: PERSONAL STRENGTHS

No one develops a positive self-concept and understands their innate strengths in isolation; it's always a reflection of the messages we've internalized through our interactions with others. A man who grew up in a household where his mother was an addict and his father often raged realized he was becoming his father in his relationship with his young children. He met with a counselor a number of times to uncover the source of his only-sometimes controlled anger, and one day, his counselor asked, "What would you expect someone to say about himself if he'd had the same childhood as yours?"

The man instantly snapped, "He'd say, 'I hate myself!'"

On a wide spectrum of experience, some of us grew up in very nurturing, happy homes, and on the other end of the spectrum, some girls have been prostituted so their parents could live on the money paid by the johns and boys have been mercilessly beaten. Most of us fall somewhere in the middle of this wide continuum, but all of us are exposed to influences that tell us we're defective, not good enough, unattractive, and "less than" in many other ways.

Beyond childhood messages, a number of other factors shape our self-concept, including our personality (some of us are naturally more reflective than others, and if the "raw material" for reflection is negative, they'll almost certainly draw negative conclusions in self-evaluation), life experiences, physical and mental health, and the impact of peers, among other factors. Thankfully, self-esteem isn't fixed. The brain's amazing neuroplasticity is our great hope for lasting change.

When we find a person to connect with us to communicate unconditional regard, we lower our guard and trust what this person says about us . . . or at least, we begin to. Gradually, we trust that what this person sees in us is real, and our self-concept shifts from threatened to affirmed, loved, and strong. At first, we're probably resistant because we don't want to be fooled and hurt again, but the consistency of the positive messages, verbal and non-verbal, slowly erodes our negative self-perception and self-doubt.

We don't need to look for a perfect person, but we need someone who won't give us simplistic answers to life's biggest struggles. I've known people who picked the wrong person, which was very discouraging, and then picked another wrong person, which was genuinely devastating. Look for someone who . . .

- Listens
- Asks second and third questions (which tells you he didn't jump to a conclusion too fast)
- Has integrity and guards personal information
- Is both honest and gracious
- Is emotionally authentic
- Is patient
- Is humble enough to say, "I don't know."
- Weeps when you weep and rejoices when you rejoice.

THE SECOND PILLAR: ENVIRONMENTAL STRENGTHS

Humans are relational beings by nature— we simply can't thrive in isolation. We simply cannot function well without a web of strong, secure, affirming relationships. We can envision our relationships in concentric circles: In the middle are one to three people who know us well. This person or these people are instrumental in the first two phases of transformational change—connecting and inspiring. The next ring is inhabited by people who are supportive, but who may come in and out of our lives, such as friends, teachers, coaches, and mentors. The third circle includes those who give us information and meet specific needs, like merchants, plumbers, doctors, attorneys, insurance agents, and financial planners. The outer ring has people who share our values even if we don't spend much time with them. We choose to work for a company or teach in a school system where we believe our ethics and values are shared. We don't need intimate relationships with all of them to appreciate our commonalities.

> Everyone needs a true friend in the center who won't judge us for being honest about our struggles.

Many people have populated the outer rings, but they have no one in the center. For a number of reasons, they haven't made these vital connections. Transparency is perceived as a threat—"What would they do if they really knew me?" so it's safer to keep people at arm's length. Everyone needs a true friend in the center who won't judge us for being honest about our struggles. If we have difficulty finding someone like that, we may need to enlist a "paid friend"—a therapist who is never surprised by anything we might disclose.

THE THIRD PILLAR: PERFORMANCE STRENGTHS

Instead of taking our abilities for granted, we need to become students of our talents, and we need to invest in sharpening them. We flourish when we use our abilities to their fullest to accomplish things we never dreamed possible. With support and inspiration from those who care for us, we build our repertoire of skills, we dream about what might be (instead of fearing what might be), and we find the courage to step into the unknown. We explore our potential and learn to navigate challenges. Our performance is a function of positive self-regard (the first pillar: "I can do it!"), a supportive environment (the second pillar: "She believes I can do it!"), and the accumulation of new experiences as we step out of our comfort zones (the third pillar: "I did it, and now I'm going to do it again . . . even better!").

Hard skills are our professional and occupational talents, and soft skills are our interpersonal strengths. Each interaction teaches us something. We become more observant—more shrewd as we see patterns in behavior yet more humble and kind because we realize we never know the whole story in someone's life. We gain insights from those who are in our inner circle. They've been down the road farther than we have, and they have insights we haven't yet acquired. They don't control us, but they may say, "I'm not going to tell you what to do, but this is what happened when I faced a situation like yours."

> **But when people feel safe and secure, they're far more willing to try something new.**

For instance, in any supervisory relationship (such as teachers with students, parents with children, bosses with employees), we can help those we lead to become more self-aware and masters of their competencies by putting them in a challenging situation and assuring them, "If you keep trying, you'll find the solution. Try different approaches and see what happens." If the person fails or gets stuck, we can provide support while at the same time prodding their sense of discovery: "It's great that you tried. What did you learn?" And when the person succeeds, we can point out more than the outcome; we can say, "When you did (this and that and the other thing), you persevered. I'm really proud of your tenacity and problem-solving!" For most of us, experimentation rarely happens outside a caring, supportive relationship. The risk of failure is simply too great. But when people feel safe and secure, they're far more willing to try something new. For the first few times, they'll probably look over their shoulders to see if they really are safe and secure, but after enough times, their brains will create new wiring so that creativity and experimentation become the new normal.

"BRAINS ON A STICK"

Much of the modern educational system and training in virtually every field of study, including counseling, focus on acquiring knowledge. It goes like this: If we gain knowledge, we should be able to think more productively, which will result in life change. But this, Professor James K. A. Smith asserts, makes people "brains on a stick." Descartes famously stated, "I think, therefore I am," but Smith's research shows that we can't think our way into life transformation. If the heart—our deepest longings and our strongest motivations—aren't moved by experience, we may fill our minds with a wealth of truth, but those truths are activated only by creating new habits, action by action.[7]

Flourishing isn't merely the product of controlling our thinking, though that's one part of it. Training and interventions that focus only on our thoughts have little staying power. We flourish in the hothouse environment of supportive relationships, so we absorb the positive regard others have for us, and their confidence in us launches us into a new world of courageous action, autonomous learning, and continuous growth. This dynamic interaction is far more effective than a single method in an attempt to produce positive change. Trying new things,

---

[7] James K. A. Smith, *You Are What You Love: The Spiritual Power of Habit* (Grand Rapids, MI: Brazos Press, 2016), p. 3.

then, uncovers strengths we didn't know we had, or at least it gives us more confidence in the ones we knew about. Success is no longer a mystery—we identify our strengths, we believe in ourselves, and we aren't afraid to try and fail. In this powerful process, we actualize our potential. A piece that's often missing (or underappreciated) is the power of encouraging yet honest people in our lives. A counselor, mentor, coach, or wise friend steps into our lives, connects with us at a heart level, challenges our mistaken assumptions, asks great questions, and affirms us as we take steps forward. If we try to develop the three pillars of strengths outside the context of rich interactions, we easily become discouraged and wonder why "it isn't working." Change comes from dynamic interaction that gives us the confidence to identify and use our strengths.

THE HUMAN FACTOR

We might use a number of different labels for the flourishing model, but one of the terms is "incarnational." Some people claim that Jesus was just a gifted teacher, but that sells Him short. He was certainly that, but much more. When I read the gospel accounts, I'm struck with the intimacy and love in His connections with people. Time after time, He engaged at a heart level to demonstrate His affection and care. The religious leaders who demanded compliance with their rules instilled fear into people, but Jesus made people feel loved and secure, He involved them in every aspect of his work, and their experience with Him revolutionized their lives.

Jesus exemplified the flourishing life, and He modeled it for those who followed Him. The principle hasn't changed. A recent study called "The Heroic Client" shows that 85 percent of positive change is the result of two factors: being in a relationship where we feel valued, inspired, respected, and connecting (work, school, etc.) with what's meaningful to the individual. In other words, affirmation and purpose. When those are present, lives are transformed the vast majority of the time. Filling our brains with information—even very interesting, insightful information—accounts for only fifteen percent of genuine change.[8] In Jesus' relationship with His closest followers, He continually made them feel special, and they followed even when they were more than a bit confused because He inspired them to pursue a purpose far bigger (infinitely bigger) than themselves.

When my son Aaron was in the fifth grade, the school invited us to interview with each of his teachers. Our first meeting was with the math teacher. He was a big, burly guy who had played professional football in the CFL, and his philosophy of life was that every person had to pull himself or herself up by the bootstraps. No coddling, no excuses. With Aaron sitting next to us, the teacher said, "Your son isn't trying. He's not putting out enough effort to see progress. He's lazy. If he would practice more, he'd be okay." It was no surprise that Aaron cried when he heard his teacher's condemnation of his character, and my wife and I were angry.

---

[8] Barry L. Duncan, Scott D. Miller, and Jacqueline A. Sparks, *The Heroic Client* (San Francisco: Jossey-Bass, 2004), p. 39.

The next meeting that night was with Aaron's social studies teacher. When we walked in, we wondered if we'd get similar treatment, but he smiled and said, "There's a test I want to show you." It was a take-home test I'd helped Aaron complete. He hadn't done very well on it, so I prepared for the worst. Instead, the teacher pointed and remarked, "Look what Aaron did on the margins of the paper." Aaron had drawn pictures all around the outside of the sheets. The teacher looked at us and announced, "Your son is very creative, very talented. He has a spark. He's a reflective thinker." After a pause (I'm pretty sure he anticipated a question about his actual coursework), he assured us, "Don't worry about the tests and the content of what we're studying. He'll do okay with all that. But I'm going to teach to his spark."

Our response to the social studies teacher was the polar opposite of our meeting with the math teacher. The ex-football player shamed Aaron because he couldn't parrot back information, but the social studies teacher understood our son, saw something wonderful in him, and was committed to bringing out the very best in him. When we got home that night, I asked Aaron why he hadn't done so well on the test. He smiled at me and remarked, "Oh, it's no big deal. I'm just giving my teacher room for improvement!"

The first teacher focused only on the content of learning; the second looked beneath and beyond Aaron's brain and into his heart—he powerfully represented the wisdom and kindness of Jesus. One crushed his spirit (and mine), and the other inspired us both. Today, many years later, Aaron still points to his social studies teacher as the one who saw his potential and cared enough to inspire him in ways that have reverberated far beyond lessons in elementary social studies. This incarnational teacher connected and inspired before he tried to build.

A lot of my speaking and consulting is in school systems, so many of my stories come from these interactions. The principles, though, also apply across the wide sweep of businesses, churches, families, and nonprofit organizations. As I've observed teachers' impact on students, I've seen that many of them measure their performance by their students' grades. I believe that's short-sighted. Studying for a test taps into short-term and long-term memory, but that's only a portion of what it means to flourish in real life. Relational, creative students may not make high grades, but they often excel as they move into adulthood.

> For many people, living with past wounds and failures is like trying to swim holding an anvil.

When I teach graduate-level psychology, I've noticed that students who are obsessed with making an A+ sometimes aren't adaptable to real-life situations. However, students who regularly make Cs often have far better social skills—they make friends at the pub or watch sports with them, they're glad to hear others' stories, and they form genuine friendships. When they graduate and become practicing therapists, they're more approachable and often very effective with their clients. They've learned enough of the concepts and techniques in class so they can apply them as they invite clients into a trusting, supportive relationship. To illustrate the point, a study compared the impact of highly trained, cognitive therapists with less trained but relational ones. By now, you won't be surprised that the ones who had less training but connected relationally were more effective in helping clients make real progress. The high-powered experts came across as "I'm the expert, you're in trouble, and I have the answer for you," but people aren't very receptive to being spoken down to. The more relational therapists humanized the process and normalized the journey from hurt to health, building connections, and inspiring hope. The principle applies to every relationship, not just those in counseling offices.

For many people, living with past wounds and failures is like trying to swim holding an anvil. They feel weighed down and the best they can do is survive another day. Yes, we need to address the past, but not alone. We need to be in a caring relationship with someone who can help us grieve the hurts and experience forgiveness for our wrongs. If the past is an anvil, we'll try to get rid of it, and we won't learn from it. There are, though, incredibly valuable lessons we can learn from the past so we can apply them today. For instance, indigenous people have been wronged by whites for generations and have suffered terribly, but when their identity is tied up in those wrongs, they can't flourish today. I tell them they should certainly be honest about the past, but it's important to apply the lessons they learn from the past to today's opportunities, to live in hope instead of resentment, and create a better future for those around them.

Each day, we intuitively answer the questions: "Who am I?" "Where do I belong?" "In what ways can my life count?" If we don't find a way to grieve past wounds, they'll remain gaping and raw, and they'll consume our thoughts. Those hurts don't just evaporate with time; in fact, they fester, so it's important to find the courage to address them in a productive way. I often recommend that people write a letter, pouring out their hearts in grief and anger, and then take the letter to a river, put it in a little box, and let it float away. This is a physical reminder that they've dealt with their painful past, permitting them to focus on the opportunities and relationships of today—without trying to carry the anvil of self-pity, resentment, shame, and fear.

The Heroic Client is an extensive study of the impact of counseling that found positive change is, to a very significant degree, dependent on two factors: First, is the person in a relationship where he or she feels valued and respected? And second, are there conversations about what's meaningful to the person? These two, seemingly simple, factors account for 85 percent of positive change.[9] Gaining knowledge is only 15 percent of change ... the rest is all about the relationship. When I read the gospel accounts of the life of Jesus, I almost laugh because the

---

9 Duncan, Miller, and Sparks, *The Heroic Client*, 39.

disciples understood so little of what Jesus taught—they constantly asked Him to explain what He'd said to the crowds, but Jesus' time, attention, and affection with them were the epitome of the two factors that change lives. Luke's history of the early church and the stories of the disciples after Jesus' resurrection tell us that these factors did, indeed, transform their lives . . . and through them, ours.

A flourishing life rests on three pillars: personal strengths of self-awareness and self-confidence, environmental strengths of supportive connections, and the acquisition of performance strengths through repeated, courageous experiences. The outcome is full-orbed well-being and the crafting of a range of competencies . . . which is another description of the flourishing advantage.

Think about it:

1) What are some ways people acquire self-awareness and self-confidence?
2) On a scale of 0 (not at all) to 10 (fully), rate your level of personal strength. Explain your answer.
3) Environmental strengths are the relationships that are life-giving—at home, at work, and everywhere we connect with people.
4) On a scale of 0 (not at all) to 10 (fully), rate your level of environmental strength. Explain your answer.
5) How would you identify and describe your performance strengths?

6) On a scale of 0 (not at all) to 10 (fully), rate your level of these strengths. Explain your answer.
7) Why does the "brain on a stick" educational system (in schools, in training employees, and at home) not work very well?
8) What are some ways we can address the past so we can get beyond it and focus on today?
9) How would you describe an "incarnational model," in which counselors, teachers, coaches, mentors, and parents follow the example of Jesus in relationships?

CHAPTER

All in Your Head

We are not the survival of the fittest. We are the survival of the nurtured.
—Louis Way, as quoted in *Survival of the Nurtured* (2016) by Lu Hanessian

In the movie, *The Sixth Sense*, psychologist Malcolm Crowe treats a young, very disturbed boy named Cole. In a famous scene, the camera closes in on Cole's terrified face as he tells Crowe, "I see dead people."[10] The dead were invisible to everyone else, but not to the perceptive boy. Those who join the journey of a flourishing life have a similar (but actually quite different) response: *We see strong, capable people*—when we look in the mirror and when we look into the faces of those around us. It's a dramatic shift of mindset.

---

10 M. Night Shyamalan, *The Sixth Sense* (Aug. 2 1999; Burbank: Hollywood Pictures).

THE FLOURISHING MINDSETS

In her groundbreaking book, *Mindset*, Stanford University psychologist Carol Dweck observes that the key factor that determines success in life isn't background, education, intelligence, or talent. A person's mindset, the approach to life's challenges, makes the most difference.[11] I've found it helpful to expand on Dweck's concept of a fixed or a growth mindset and identify four: surviving, protecting, striving, and thriving (Figure 5).

Figure 5: The Four Flourishing Mindsets

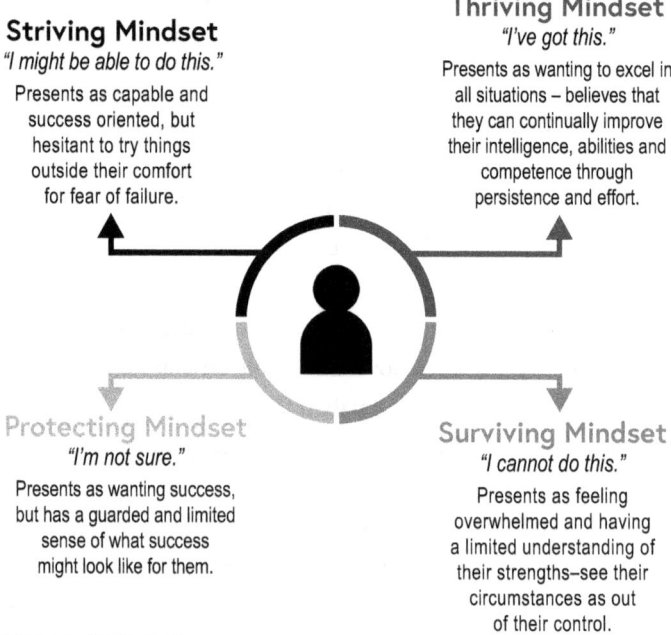

Striving Mindset
"I might be able to do this."
Presents as capable and success oriented, but hesitant to try things outside their comfort for fear of failure.

Thriving Mindset
"I've got this."
Presents as wanting to excel in all situations – believes that they can continually improve their intelligence, abilities and competence through persistence and effort.

Protecting Mindset
"I'm not sure."
Presents as wanting success, but has a guarded and limited sense of what success might look like for them.

Surviving Mindset
"I cannot do this."
Presents as feeling overwhelmed and having a limited understanding of their strengths–see their circumstances as out of their control.

---

11 Carol Dweck, PhD, *Mindset* (New York: Ballantine Books, 2016), p. 6.

1) Surviving

Some people have endured such heartache and had such little comfort and support that their present goal is to simply make it through the day. They avoid challenges because they don't have the emotional bandwidth to handle risks. They react to any perceived slight like they have a broken arm and even a slight tap on it is tremendously painful. They live with vivid memories of their painful past, or they've become numb to the past and the present. Their bucket of sorrow and fear is filled to the brim, so they have very little capacity to deal with new problems or opportunities. They are hyper-sensitive and hyper-vigilant, with finely tuned antennae to read every expression on every person to see if a threat is present. They are so guarded that they sometimes assume even a friend's casual remark is an attack.

2) Protecting

Some people are engaged but wary. Their lived experience has taught them that trust is dangerous, so they're very slow to let their guard down. Much of the time, they're pleasant and competent enough at work, with friends, and at home, but they have a very low tension tolerance, so they react when they feel pushed out of their comfort zone. They fear being seen as defective or deficient, so they're quick to find excuses or blame others for their mistakes and failures.

3) Striving

Many people are dedicated to proving they're valuable. They work hard to demonstrate their competence, and they make sure others appreciate (or at least become aware of) their contributions. They may take unreasonable risks, or they may avoid risks altogether. At work, their bosses appreciate their diligence, but their co-workers often can tell there's an insecurity behind their drive to perform.

4) Thriving

These people have effectively rewritten their stories so their past is now a springboard to more growth instead of a dark cloud over their lives. Their self-worth is no longer dependent on their success or the approval of others. They look for opportunities to try new things, and they've learned to adapt to changing circumstances. They live with a blend of self-reliance and strong relationships. Their purpose is no longer only self-focused; they invest their considerable wisdom and skills in others to help them thrive.

Each of us has a default mindset, but mindsets aren't locked in stone; they're fluid. On one day, a person may be functioning very effectively at work or at home with a striving mindset of getting things done, but a misunderstanding at work the next day sends him back into the defensiveness and self-justification of the protecting mindset. When the problem is resolved (at least well enough), the person returns to striving. The goal, of course, is to move toward thriving and incorporate those traits so that it becomes the new default mode.

In the mid-2000s, my mother and father died in quick succession. The loss was a huge blow to me. Before they died, I'd been thriving probably 80 percent of the time, but in almost an instant, I reverted all the way to surviving. For two or three months, I was rocked back on my emotional and psychological heels.

I don't look at people with surviving, protecting, and striving mindsets as defective. They're simply living by the lessons life has taught them. Their attitudes, beliefs, feelings, and actions make perfect sense in light of their experiences. I don't condemn them, I don't blame them, and I'm not annoyed by them. They're doing the very best they can ... but they don't have to stay that way. They need to find someone who connects with them and inspires them to see their lives from a different perspective. With that support, they can build new habits of thinking and acting, and become empowered with a conviction to maximize their strengths.

As human beings, we have a unique capacity to move toward a thriving mindset: our incredible brains.

THE BRAIN SCIENCE OF POSITIVE CHANGE

We may assume we can't change, we may believe that we're forever trapped in self-defeating thoughts, feelings, and choices, and we may have concluded that the past must be a prologue for our futures, but if that's what we believe, we're wrong. Our brains are wonderfully constructed to change. The brain science of positive change is a fascinating field that explores how our brains adapt, grow, and rewire in response to various experiences and interventions aimed at fostering well-being, resilience, and personal growth. Here are some key insights into the brain science of positive change:

Wired for Survival

The brain we have today was actually designed to cope with the stresses our ancestors experienced ten to twenty thousand years ago. It follows a safety-first policy, constantly scanning our surroundings four to five times a second looking for a threat. Although the brain is a very complex system, two important parts, the amygdala and hippocampus, constantly evaluate sensory information.

In chapter 1, we looked briefly at the function of the amygdala. Here, we'll examine brain function in more detail. Understanding the role of the amygdala and hippocampus is crucial for rewiring our brain for success because these brain structures play key roles in emotional regulation, memory formation, and learning processes.

Amygdala: The amygdala is involved in processing emotions, particularly fear and stress responses. When faced with challenges or setbacks, our amygdala can become overactive, leading to heightened stress levels and impaired decision-making. By understanding how the amygdala operates, we can learn to regulate our emotional responses to stressors, enabling us to stay focused, make better decisions, and effectively navigate challenges on the path to success.

Hippocampus: The hippocampus is primarily associated with memory formation and spatial navigation. It plays a crucial role in learning and retaining new information. By understanding how the hippocampus processes and stores memories, we can optimize our learning strategies to enhance memory consolidation and recall. This is essential for acquiring new skills, knowledge, and experiences that contribute to personal and professional success.

Figure 6: The Role of the Amygdala and Hippocampus

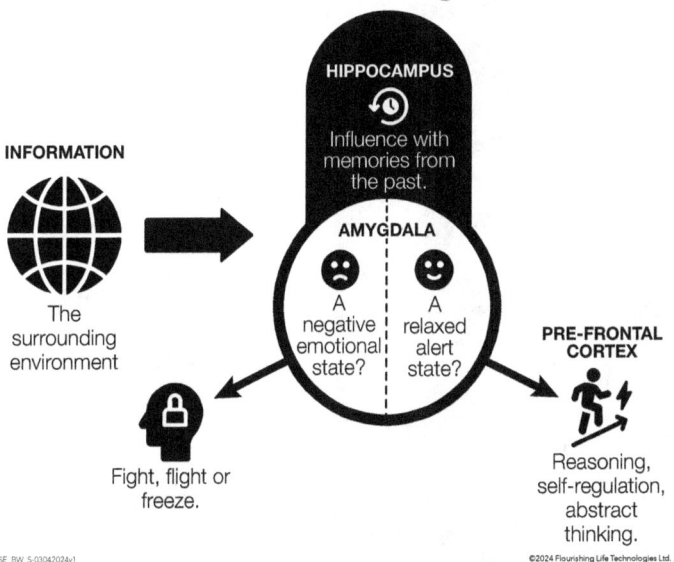

Both the amygdala and hippocampus are involved in the brain's neuroplasticity, the ability to reorganize and form new neural connections in response to experiences and environmental stimuli. This means that by actively engaging in activities that challenge and stimulate these brain regions, such as mindfulness practices, cognitive-behavioral therapies, and strategic learning

84 THE FLOURISHING ADVANTAGE

techniques, we can promote positive changes in our brain structure and function. On the other hand, if we have challenging lived experiences, our brains can become over-sensitized to perceived dangers that dictate our fear-based defensive responses.

Figure 7: The Threat and Safety Responses

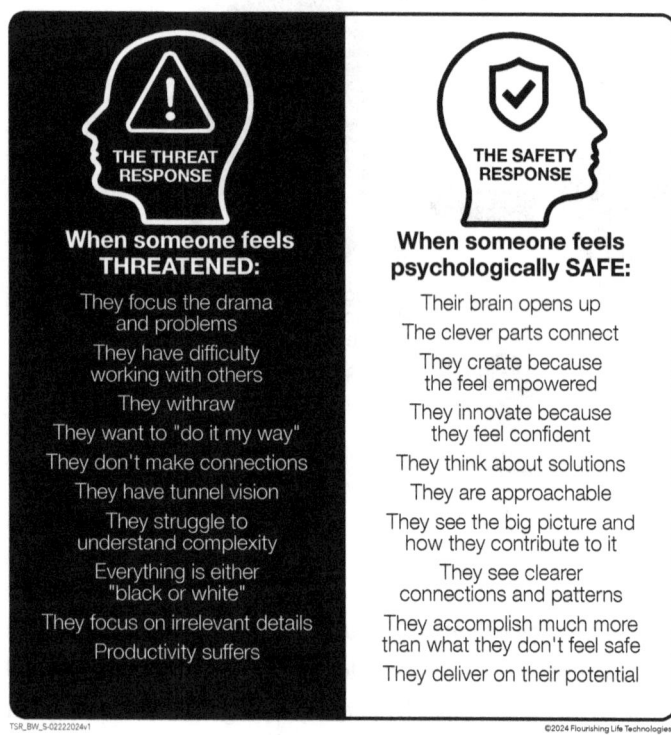

Making Connections

As people make meaningful connections with supportive people, they feel less threatened, and their amygdala can calm down. Then, hormones are released in the limbic system, enabling people to distinguish between harmful and helpful experiences. The limbic and neocortex are then activated so people ask, "What did I do to contribute to this painful event?" and "What did I do that helped produce this pleasure?" This process establishes a memory, and the prefrontal cortex, the brain's executive function, then analyzes the event and the things that contributed to it.

> Taking action—and learning from the experience—is what changes the brain.

Experience is the great teacher. Knowledge is important, but there are plenty of very bright, well-informed people who are only surviving. Taking action—and learning from the experience—is what changes the brain. It's about stepping out of our comfort zone with courage and grace to embrace the unknown in the context of supportive and caring people.

Neuroplasticity

The brain has an amazing ability to reorganize its structure, functions, and connections in response to learning, experience, and environmental changes. The brain can change throughout a person's life by introducing new lived experiences that are growth-focused and transformative. This is crucial for positive change because individuals can acquire new skills, recover from injuries, and adapt to new circumstances, all of which contribute to personal growth and well-being.

Rewiring through Experience

Experiences, both positive and negative, have the potential to reshape the brain. Positive experiences, such as learning a new skill, practicing gratitude, or experiencing joy, can strengthen neural pathways associated with well-being. Cultivating positive experiences can promote brain changes that enhance emotional regulation, resilience, and overall mental health. This can lead to a more positive and fulfilling life. An article in *Psychology Today* explains:

> *The brain changes most rapidly in* childhood, *but it's now clear that the brain continues to develop throughout life. At any time, day-to-day behaviors can have measurable effects on brain structure and function. For example, a well-known study of British taxi drivers found that memorizing the city streets led to changes in the memory center, the hippocampus, and that those who had driven for longer had more expansion in the hippocampus. These changes in middle age highlight the role of neuroplasticity in learning across the lifespan.*[12]

---

[12] "Neuroplasticity," *Psychology Today*, https://www.psychologytoday.com/us/basics/neuroplasticity.

ALL IN YOUR HEAD 87

Dopamine and oxytocin

Dopamine is a neurotransmitter associated with reward and motivation. When we experience success or a sense of accomplishment, our brain releases dopamine, reinforcing positive behaviors. Developing a growth mindset triggers the release of dopamine when individuals overcome challenges or achieve their goals. This positive reinforcement encourages them to continue striving for personal growth and flourishing. Oxytocin is sometimes called "the love hormone" because it promotes trust, vulnerability, and sexual pleasure. One expert said it's the antidote to amygdala hijacking: instead of "fight or flight," oxytocin heightens a "tend and befriend" response.[13]

Mindfulness and Meditation

These practices have been shown to induce structural and functional changes in the brain. Regular mindfulness practice, like meditation, can increase gray matter density in brain regions associated with self-awareness and emotional regulation. These changes can lead to reduced stress, improved focus, and enhanced emotional well-being, contributing to personal growth and positive change.

Social connections

Social interactions and relationships can have a profound impact on brain function. Positive social experiences, like emotional support and close relationships, can lead to the release of oxytocin, a hormone, as we've seen, associated with bonding

---

13 Shelley E. Taylor, *Psychological Science*, Vol. 18, No. 11, pp. 965-970.

and trust. Building and nurturing positive social connections can improve mental health, reduce feelings of isolation, and promote a sense of belonging and well-being.

Learning and cognitive growth

Learning new skills, acquiring knowledge, and challenging the brain through intellectual pursuits can stimulate the growth of new neurons and the formation of new synaptic connections. Lifelong learning not only keeps the brain engaged but also contributes to cognitive vitality and adaptability, which are essential for personal growth and maintaining mental acuity as people age.

Positive Psychology Interventions

Interventions such as gratitude exercises, acts of kindness, and setting and achieving meaningful goals, have been linked to changes in brain function and structure. Engaging in these interventions can lead to increased happiness, greater life satisfaction, and improved mental health, all of which support positive personal change.

Stress Reduction and Resilience

Chronic stress can have detrimental effects on the brain, while stress reduction techniques like mindfulness and relaxation exercises can help restore normal brain function. Learning to manage and reduce stress contributes to improved mental health, emotional resilience, and the capacity for positive change as the brain is more adaptive in response to challenges.

The brain's capacity for positive change is grounded in its remarkable ability to adapt and rewire itself throughout our lives. By engaging in activities and practices that promote well-being, resilience, and personal growth, we can harness the power of neuroplasticity to lead more fulfilling lives. Understanding the brain science of positive change underscores the importance of adopting practical, effective strategies and behaviors that support mental and emotional well-being. Then, feelings of anxiety don't overwhelm us and stop us in our tracks; instead, our new brain wiring interprets the challenge as an opportunity to step out of our comfort zone, and our brains kick into a problem-solving gear.

This is a crucial point: no one makes progress by hearing a talk or reading a book.

Of course, those whose default mode is surviving have more work to get all the way to thriving, but as many of the stories in this book show, it's certainly possible. Gradually, as they process their emotions more effectively and make bold, life-affirming choices in the context of supportive relationships, they have more positive life experiences, which form the foundation of further growth.

This is a crucial point: no one makes progress by hearing a talk or reading a book (even this one!). Becoming a person with a thriving mindset happens when courageous choices produce positive experiences, and each of these slightly changes our neural pathways. Neuroplasticity is our hope for real change. Talks, podcasts, books, sermons, and talk therapy have their place in giving us knowledge, but as we've seen, change doesn't happen until we put that knowledge into action. We have a natural resistance to change because the "good ideas" others give us don't connect with our lived experience. But when we're in a relationship of love, understanding, and trust, oxytocin floods our minds and hearts with affirmation, making the impossible seem more probable. Then, when we take steps and experience progress, dopamine reinforces our courage with the sensation of pleasure. This is the kind of feedback loop that changes lives!

The primary job of the parent, teacher, mentor, and coach isn't to disseminate golden truths; it's to connect with people so powerfully that their ideas go far deeper and make a far greater impact. Children, students, and friends may have entered the relationship with very little courage, but they "borrow the courage" of those who are inspiring them.

HOW CHANGE HAPPENS

It's helpful to put the concepts together that we've explored so far. People can make real progress from their current mode—surviving, protecting, or striving—to genuinely thriving by being in a relationship with at least one person who connects with them, inspires them, encourages them to build powerful new habits, and empowers them to a high level of competence. As Figure 8 demonstrates, we can envision this interaction like this.

Figure 8: The Flourishing Mindset Model

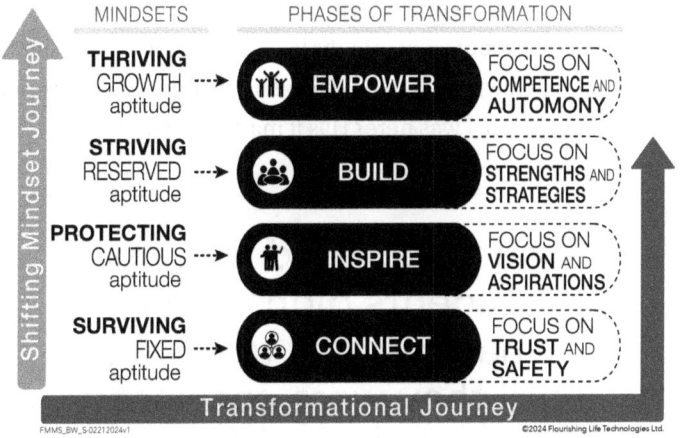

The responsibility of your parent, teacher, coach, or mentor is to create a hothouse environment where you can grow by focusing on trust and safety, then being inspired by dreams and aspirations, then building strengths and discovering new strategies, and finally, enjoying a high level of competence and autonomy. Your responsibility is to be open-minded and open-hearted, trust the person and the process, and take courageous steps so new neural pathways are created.

Not long ago I spoke to a school board to share the concepts of flourishing. I explained that the teachers are the greatest asset in the school system—not the new computers, not a brilliant curriculum, not the athletic department, and not the facilities. Why? Because teachers have relationships with students, and relationships are the indispensable key to a thriving, flourishing life. Kids learn best when they feel safe and respected, so connecting with them is the first and foremost essential.

I went back about eight months later to speak at a professional development day, and I asked, "What has been your experience since the last time I was here? Has it made a difference?"

> **She discovered that her students didn't value what she was teaching until they were convinced she valued them.**

Instantly, a teacher stood up and spoke loudly so everyone could hear, "Wayne, when you spoke a few months ago, I thought you were the biggest jerk I'd ever been around. Who are you to tell me how I should teach?" (Some teachers gasped; others laughed nervously.) She smiled and said, "But I tried some of the things you suggested. To be honest, I was exhausted, on the verge of burnout. I was reacting to everything the kids in my class were doing, and not in a good way. I didn't like my job, and I hadn't liked it for eighteen years. When I tried some of the things you talked about, I connected with the kids. For the first time since I graduated from college, I enjoy coming to school every day. I even like the kids now!" (Lots of laughs now.) "And they like coming to my class. Your idea of putting relationships before learning works. I'm your test case. The change isn't because the kids changed; it's because I changed first."

This teacher had been in surviving mode for eighteen years, but in only a few months, she moved all the way to thriving. She discovered that her students didn't value what she was teaching until they were convinced she valued them. She had become a teacher because she wanted to have a positive impact on students, but in a short time, the stress of trying to control kids sapped her energy, undermined her purpose, and made her see students as adversaries. Her perspective changed, which changed her attitude and behavior. The kids had been trying to get their needs met all along, but they didn't have someone they trusted to help them find good ways to meet them. When she connected with them in a way that built trust, everything changed. When they were excited about coming to a class where they felt valued, learning became an inevitable byproduct.

Can you relate to this teacher? Have you ever begun with an inspiring vision but through failure, opposition, or the grind of life found yourself only surviving? Do you hate your job and your life feels empty? If you've moved past that phase, it's almost certainly because someone came into your world to give you a foundation of trust and safety. Your vision was rekindled, you could focus on your strengths instead of being weighed down by memories of failure, and you began to feel better about yourself—you felt confident that you have what it takes, and you're fulfilling your highest ambitions.

Or can you relate to the students? Have you tried to get your needs met, but you seem to just dig a deeper hole for yourself? What difference would it make for you to feel safe and valued? Has someone stepped into your life to connect with you? If not, where can you find someone like that?

When you feel safe, you can dream again. The protecting phase is still defensive, but it's more productive than just surviving. You're repeating behaviors that work, but you're not trying anything new. As you find the courage to experiment, you'll uncover unknown strengths (or you'll enhance strengths you knew you had). As you develop a track record of bold choices and learn from your successes and failures, you'll feel empowered, you'll adapt to different circumstances, and you'll be on an upward trajectory of continual growth. It all starts with feeling valued.

In the next four chapters, we'll look more closely at the four phases of transformational change: connect, inspire, build, and empower.

Think about it:
1) How would you describe the feelings, motivations, attitudes, and behaviors of people who have each of the four mindsets?
    - Surviving
    - Protecting

- Striving
- Thriving

2) Draw a timeline of your life, from birth to today. Note the significant blocks of time, for instance: childhood, high school, higher education, early years of career and marriage, children, job changes, moves, etc. Which of the four mindsets did you have in each of those blocks of time?
3) What is the evidence of the mindsets in each period?
4) Does the concept of neuroplasticity give you hope for real transformation? Explain your answer.
5) What difference does it make (or will it make) for you to realize that reading and talking aren't enough to promote genuine change, and what works is a new pattern of courageous, lived experiences?

CHAPTER
5

Connect

Deep transformational change is never transactional. It is always relational.
—Aiko Bethea on the Dare to Lead with Brené Brown podcast (Nov. 9, 2020)

In my observations over the years, I've seen two kinds of people: those who are living with a secure identity as someone who is loved and valued ... and those who are desperately trying to earn, if not love, at least respect. The second group has internalized messages of being "not enough," "less than," "don't bother ...," and "you'd better ..." They view themselves as unworthy of love and respect, so they don't treat themselves with kindness and affirmation. In other words, the lack of meaningful, positive connections with others has created a lack of meaningful, positive opinions of themselves. Earlier we talked about the importance of "borrowed courage"; here, we're borrowing and absorbing the way others view us. Living with the gnawing need to be seen, loved, and respected doesn't end when we develop more sophisticated coping strategies so we look like we have it all together. We want a loving relationship with our spouse, we want meaningful times with our kids, and we long to be comfortable in social settings instead of constantly fearful we'll say the wrong thing and look foolish, but if we don't like ourselves, these genuine hopes are seldom satisfied.

The obsession with our deficiencies continues until we form the kind of affirming connections we've needed all our lives. And it's never too late to find and form these connections.

A man, I'll call him Bill, told me he's jealous of a friend who talks freely and gladly about his relationship with his parents and siblings. "His dad took him fishing, told him stories, and was his best friend when he was growing up. And his brothers . . . they were each other's biggest fans!" Bill related wistfully. But Bill had a very different experience with his family: "My dad was an alcoholic, and my mother was perpetually angry—at him, at my brother and me because we didn't do everything exactly the way she demanded, and I think she was angry with God for letting her husband ruin their lives." Bill absorbed the message that his father didn't care about him and he could never do enough to please his mother. Feelings of abandonment and the fear of ridicule haunted him for years . . . until he asked his friend to spend more time with him so he could feel what it's like to be safe and valued. It took some time, but this connection made a world of difference in Bill's life.

A lot of my work with people is helping them uncover the source of their self-abandonment, and in some cases, self-loathing. I ask simply, "Where do you think those feelings and perceptions came from?" Some have such repressed emotions and selective memories that they can't readily put the pieces of the past and present together, but most people can connect the dots with a little help.

> Progress begins when we start to believe we're people of value.

When we see ourselves through the eyes of God, we walk a little taller—not because we've impressed him with our performance or manipulated him by our wiles, but only because he sees inherent value in us.

Progress begins when we start to believe we're people of value. This perception is "more caught than taught," so it's crucial to be in a relationship with someone who knows the worst about you and loves you still. No hiding. No excuses. A safe person doesn't laugh, ridicule, or run away when we dare to talk about our deepest hurts and fears. However, accurate teaching is a helpful component in changing our self-regard and the myriad of implications in our relationships. The Bible tells us that we were created "in the image of God." That doesn't mean, as Archie Bunker once commented in *All in the Family,* that "God looks like me."[14] It means that God has imparted qualities that make us separate from the rest of creation. We are uniquely valuable to him. These qualities are tarnished by our innate selfishness, but they're still present in every person on the planet. When we see ourselves through the eyes of God, we walk a little taller—not because we've impressed him with our performance or manipulated him by our wiles, but only because he sees inherent value in us.

ATTACHMENT INSIGHTS

An article from the perspective of positive psychology identifies attachment theory as a helpful model for understanding the importance of connections. John Bowlby was a psychoanalyst who noticed how separation affected small children, and later as the effects became normalized, when they became adults. He identified four attachment styles:

1) Secure attachment

These people see others as supportive and see themselves as competent and worthy of respect. They engage easily with others, trust wisely, and display creative problem-solving and resilience when faced with challenges.

2) Anxious-avoidant attachment

These people lack self-confidence and have little trust that others have their best interests in mind. Their deeply rooted fear

---

14 *All in the Family,* John Rich, Bob LaHendro, H. Wesley Kenney, and Paul Bogart (January 12, 1971; New York, NY: CBS), Television.

causes them to withdraw from any hint of tension, so they have only superficial relationships, even in marriage and parenting. Their goal is to reduce their level of anxiety by emotionally hiding or using anger to keep people away.

3) Anxious-resistant attachment

The insecurity of these people brings out a very different reaction than the anxious-avoidant people. They cling to powerful people with the hope that they will protect them, but they steer away from meaningful peer relationships.

4) Disorganized attachment

As the label implies, these insecure people haven't developed a clear coping strategy. Sometimes they isolate, but other times they bully or are disruptive to get attention.[15]

> Left on our own, none of us would value ourselves. We must experience it from others, bathe in it, and let it seep deep into our souls.

These four descriptions aren't offered to heap shame on those who haven't felt valued but to offer insights about the ways we try

---

[15] Courtney E. Ackerman, "What Is Attachment Theory? Bowlby's 4 Stages Explained," *PositivePsychology.com*, 27 Apr. 2018, https://positivepsychology.com/attachment-theory/.

to make sense of our past, painful experiences. Growth begins with insight, and in this case, the need to form secure attachments with a few people (or at least one person). Then, change happens from the inside out. When we feel valued, we don't operate to prove ourselves or impress people; feeling valued and secure brings out the very best in us. Left on our own, none of us would value ourselves. We must experience it from others, bathe in it, and let it seep deep into our souls. This connection is the first and fundamental essential for human flourishing. When we don't feel valued, we're driven to prove ourselves by our performance, please people to win their approval, or hide from risks because we already feel too vulnerable (and often we vacillate among the three). But when we're secure, we can look up and look out, inspired to try new things and make a difference in our world.

MOVING PAST SURVIVING

People with a surviving mindset are often double-minded—desperate for relationships but terrified of being vulnerable. They feel stuck. They view their current condition and their lack of aptitude to change as immutable. Any mistake is a threat, and any criticism is like a dagger to the heart. For that reason, they avoid any risks of failure, so they don't embrace life's challenges. When they fail, they quickly minimize ("It wasn't that bad."), excuse ("I couldn't help it."), or blame others ("Hey, it's not my fault!"). They may become perfectionists to avoid the risk of failure and ridicule, or they may give up on even trying. A surviving mindset severely limits their involvement in meaningful relationships and prevents professional growth.

Change starts with connecting. Those in a surviving mindset need to feel safe and valued before they will take the risk of engaging in growth activities. All learning and social development is based on establishing a relationship of empathy, integrity, and affirmation. The steps of change include:

1) Identify the roadblocks. Are you...

   ... Focused on just getting through the day?

   ... Avoiding meaningful interaction because you feel too vulnerable?

   ... Avoiding challenges and opportunities because the risk of failure is too great?

   ... Feeling threatened by situations that require skills and insights beyond your perceived ability?

   ... Afraid of failure or being hurt by criticism?

   ... Withdrawing from people and situations that make you feel overwhelmed?

   ... Finding comfort in low expectations?

2) Engage with someone you learn to trust. Will you take the step to...

   ... Begin to tell your story (your real story) to the person you're beginning to trust?

   ... Talk to that person about the goals and expectations of your relationship?

   ... Trust that overtures of kindness are genuine?

   ... Learn to feel more comfortable with affirmation?

... Fight your natural resistance to being known?

... Stay engaged when you feel uncomfortable telling more of your story?

3) Stay connected. Will you ...

... Explain to the person what it means for you to feel safe and valued?

... Share how you feel about the relationship as it progresses?

... Ask for help as you begin to take risks?

... Be honest about what you need from the person?

... Continually redefine your identity and your purpose in light of feeling safer and more secure?

... Embrace new possibilities as you're inspired to try new things?

The importance of having strong, secure connections never ends. As people move from a surviving mindset to protecting, that's real progress, and they need encouragement and support for each step. Then, as they enter the striving phase, taking risks to step out of their comfort zones will become more natural, but they need encouragement and insight to learn to take risks wisely. As they move toward thriving, supportive relationships will mean more than ever. Now, their mentors become peers, and they encourage each other to grow even more each day.

EVEN THEM, EVEN YOU

People who have suffered significant trauma, abuse, and neglect often long for connections but push people away because they find it very hard to trust that anyone genuinely cares for them. A friend's daughter, we'll call her Becca, was a vibrant young woman who lived abroad for several years. During a span of about six months, she witnessed six people run over and killed by buses. The country where Becca was living didn't have a Good Samaritan law, so no one stepped in to help those who were dying in front of them. She was shattered by the experience. When she returned home, she was surly and distant, even from those who dearly loved her. Her family and close friends wondered if she'd ever be happy and confident again. But Becca let one friend into the darkness of her heart, and gradually, the love, understanding, and compassion she received brought her back from surviving to protecting to striving and finally to thriving.

I've noticed that people who have recently immigrated from troubled homelands at first look for the basics of food and housing, but when these needs are met, they wander like they're in a fog, wondering what to do and where to go. Those who connect with someone—perhaps someone from their country who has been here for a while and has settled into a rhythm of life, perhaps a social worker, or perhaps people from a local church or nonprofit organization—experience the support they desperately need and begin to find their way in a strange land. When they've told me their stories, I'm often impressed with their resilience and their commitment to taking their families to a better life. During the migration, they showed remarkable courage and creativity to get to our country, but then they reverted to survival mode, trying just to make it through the day. When they feel the security of new connections, their strengths can surface again, and often, the new challenges of living in a new country bring out strengths they didn't even know they had. For these people, the process of moving from surviving to protecting to striving goes fairly quickly because their lived experience tells them it's possible. Thriving is a bigger challenge because the best they could do in their home countries was striving.

During the Covid epidemic, many people were rocked back on their emotional, psychological, and relational heels. They were thrown off balance by the conflicting messages about the vaccines, lockdowns, and supply chain shortages. Many of us felt deeply threatened—not only by the disease but by alarmists—and reverted to surviving and protecting. We saw those who didn't agree with us as enemies, and our culture became polarized. Many of us lost our resilience (or never had it, but we didn't know it until the stress of the epidemic). We also lost our ability to see those who disagreed with us as reasonable people who simply have a different perspective. Even if we didn't say angry things *to* people, we said them *about* people. The lockdowns, masks, and the atmosphere of fear contributed to our sense of isolation. Even if we wanted to connect with people to give and receive support, it was difficult if not impossible. Hopefully, the government health officials and all the rest of us will handle it better next time. People in every age group need affirming human connections all the time. We can't afford to let anything—even a pandemic—block our most influential relationships.

When I talk to people, some of them tell me about troubled relationships at home or at work. When I ask about their past experiences with people, they often tell heartbreaking stories of abandonment and various forms of abuse. I help them connect the dots so they see that their present difficulties may be the result of a deficit of love and support in the past, and that they simply can't draw water from an empty well. Supportive, encouraging connections are the lifeblood of a flourishing life. They can't be neglected, and the need shouldn't be overlooked. They make our lives worth living.

Think about it:
1) What are some signs someone is in surviving mode?
2) How would you characterize their relationships?
3) Who has been the person who has connected with you most powerfully and positively? Describe the person's impact on you.
4) Which attachment style best describes your childhood? Explain your answer.
5) How has that style shown up in your life as an adult?
6) The action points at the end of the chapter are "identify the need," "engage," and "stay connected." Look at those sections and write a plan for finding and benefitting from being connected with a supportive person.

CHAPTER

6

Inspire

The best way to predict the future is to create it.
—Peter Drucker

When you trust someone who has connected with you, that person has the opportunity to inspire you. Connecting answers the *who* question; inspiration points you to the *what*, *why*, and *how*. With a sense of purpose, an appreciation of your strengths, and a shot of confidence from someone you trust, virtually all things are possible.

When we focus primarily on our deficits, we're relegated to merely surviving or protecting, but when we have a new foundation of hope, we form a bigger, better picture of tomorrow, and we look for every opportunity to take steps to get there. Inspiration enables us to reframe our life's stories. We no longer interpret our past wounds and failures as debilitating but as hard lessons we need to learn. Before, we felt stuck, hopeless, and helpless. We didn't reach for new possibilities because we assumed we'd fail again and become the object of jokes. But now, with greater confidence instilled in us by our mentor, the past no longer defines us.

People who have suffered domestic abuse have difficulty moving beyond their identity as a victim because it has been so deeply rooted in their self-image. When they get away from the abuser for a while, many of them can't imagine life without that cruel person. They've connected, but with the wrong person. In fact, most don't ever leave because they've been told the abuse would be even worse if they walked out the door. Terror shackles them to the abuser. A national domestic violence organization explains:

> *A victim's reasons for staying with their abusers are extremely complex and, in most cases, are based on the reality that their abuser will follow through with the threats they have used to keep them trapped: the abuser will hurt or kill them, they will hurt or kill the kids, they will win custody of the children, they will harm or kill pets or others, they will ruin their victim financially —the list goes on. The victim in violent relationships knows their abuser best and fully knows the extent to which they will go to make sure they have and can maintain control over the victim. The victim literally may not be able to safely escape or protect those they love.*[16]

---
[16] "Why Do Victims Stay?" *NCADV.*

"A recent study of intimate partner homicides found 20% of homicide victims were not the domestic violence victims themselves, but family members, friends, neighbors, persons who intervened, law enforcement responders, or bystanders."[17]

When I've worked with women who have suffered harm from a partner or spouse, some of them have told me, "When I'm with him, at least I feel something. I don't know what it feels like to be loved. As a matter of fact, it scares me. I don't know who I am apart from him." Sometimes, admitting they've made a terrible mistake in staying with the abuser is too much shame to bear. Even if they leave, many of them are magnetically drawn to another person who treats them with contempt. Why? Because it's so familiar and they think they know how to cope with this kind of relationship.

Responding to our mentor's inspiring messages requires faith ... that our mentor knows more about our opportunities in the future than we do, that our doubts can be overcome by renewed trust, and life can, indeed, be much richer than we've ever experienced. When we take those steps of faith and experience progress, brain science becomes our ally, and new neural pathways are established.

Connecting and inspiring are the cornerstones of a firm foundation for a flourishing life. If people start with the build phase to implement their strengths in new strategies without first having

---

[17] Sharon G. Smith, Katherine A. Fowler, and Phyllis H. Niolon, "Intimate Partner Homicide and Corollary Victims in 16 States: National Violent Death Reporting System, 2003-2009," *American Public Health Associations (AJPH),* 104, no. 3 (March 2014): abstract, as quoted in "Why Do Victims Stay?" by *NCADV*.

this foundation, they soon become discouraged, scattered in their activities, or run on empty long enough that they burn out. Problem-solving is important, but it works best when people feel safe and valued, and they've spent time reframing their stories so the inevitable setbacks and disappointments don't connect (or don't connect as strongly) with haunting memories of past failures.

Many therapeutic models and leadership training begin with identifying the problem and then enlisting strengths and finding new strategies. Those are perfectly fine, right, and good, as long as the person is building on a solid foundation. When people have the strong support of someone who believes in them and can connect new strategies with a self-generated, inspired purpose, most of the therapeutic and leadership models will work well. But that's not what happens in most cases. A good foundation of support and inspiration opens doors of imagination for people to dream, explore creative solutions, ask good questions, reinterpret their past experiences, and patiently begin to write a new story.

Many years ago when I was young, I worked as a laborer with some Italian masons in Toronto. They spent a lot of time digging the footings and getting the corners of the foundation exactly right . . . so much time that I wondered if we'd ever start laying bricks. One day, the foreman must have noticed my impatience. He told me, "Wayne, if we don't get the cornerstones right, everything else will be out of whack." I've remembered his comment all these years because I've seen its application in the lives of people who are in the phases of surviving and protecting. Some are immobilized by fear and doubt, but others frantically search for the next idea, strategy, or tool that will give them the meaning and success they crave. Without exception, they're deeply discouraged when one doesn't work, and even more discouraged with each subsequent failure.

POSSIBILITIES

The phase of inspiration calls us to move out of our cautious, protective comfort zones. Before, every risk looked like Mt. Everest, an impossible mountain to climb. We looked through the lens of shame, and we were sure failure was around the next corner again. Shame crushes the soul. There's a distinct difference between guilt and shame: Guilt is the sense that we've done something wrong; shame is the conviction that we're irredeemably flawed. Dr. Karl Menninger put shame in the context of other destructive emotions: "The voice of the intelligence is drowned out by the roar of fear. It is ignored by the voice of desire. It is contradicted by the voice of shame. It is biased by hate and extinguished by anger. Most of all it is silenced by ignorance."[18]

People who are surviving or protecting often live under a cloud of shame. They feel deeply broken, hopeless, helpless, and worthless. They believe their past is a sure predictor of the future. Feeling valued and being inspired cut out the heart of shame. They are the antidote to feeling worthless and hopeless. No, deeply held negative conclusions of ourselves don't magically evaporate in one conversation, but they can *begin* to

---
18 Dr. Karl Menninger, *The Progressive*, October 1955.

evaporate and be replaced with a single conversation. We need sounding boards to mitigate our fear of failure so we can take a risk and try something new.

> It's only when knowledge is put into action by trying something new and repeating the action that change happens.

The growth pattern is: we identify a risk, we muster the required courage to step into it, we interpret success or failure as a positive learning experience, and our brains make a subtle but significant change that reinforces our confidence. This is where the "aha!" happens. I hear people say things like, "I had no idea that I didn't have to stay stuck in that dead-end job. I could have changed jobs long ago, but this was the time. I'm more challenged and more fulfilled... and I'm making more money now!"

As I've mentioned, gaining knowledge doesn't necessarily result in change. It's only when knowledge is put into action by trying something new and repeating the action that change happens.

My story is a good example. I was a colossal failure in school until a professor stepped into my life and believed in me. His faith in me and my future was crucial, but it wasn't enough. He inspired me to think differently, to believe change was possible, but even that wasn't enough. Real change happened when I took action based on borrowed courage and confidence. My comfort zone was a strong belief that I was deficient—life wasn't good and it was never going to be any better. (The term "comfort zone" can be misleading. It doesn't mean it's a pleasant state of mind; it's only that we avoid risks. For me, my comfort zone was a kind of prison, and I had lost hope of ever getting out. I had become comfortable with the pain, fear, and doubt, and I couldn't imagine living without them. They were my constant companions.) The professor taught me that my anxiety and fear could become my teachers instead of my prison guards. I could learn from those feelings. They were teaching me to try something different instead of living with them. Of course, I threw up a lot of excuses and rationalizations, insisting that nothing would work and that I was doomed, but he patiently and persistently communicated love, support, and confidence in me.

I'd like to report that the dramatic change happened quickly for me, but that's not the case. It took ten years, from when I was seventeen until I was twenty-seven. The professor opened my eyes to notice other people who were courageously moving out of their comfort zones, taking risks, and enjoying new possibilities. Eventually, I saw two options: to take the risk of stepping out and failing, which would result in my biggest fear of looking foolish to other people, or taking the easy way out and staying stuck. I realized I was already a failure. Staying there would only reinforce that fact. I found the courage to face my fear and do what was right for me. I applied to a college, but they turned me down. The message screamed, "You're not our type of student!"

The professor insisted, "Wayne, you can learn, and I can teach you to learn."

I put my fear aside and replied, "I'm willing to trust you."

He ushered me into a learning zone. I found that if I applied my strengths and the new skills he taught me, and repeated them again and again, I entered the growth zone. In other words, I found new ways to be successful. Then, the big challenge came. I applied again to college and went there to take an entrance exam. I was terrified. What if I failed this time, after all I'd gone through and after all the professor had invested in me? But I passed, and a huge door opened in front of me.

As I attended classes that first year, I was twenty-seven, and the students sitting around me were seventeen and eighteen years old. I studied twice as much as they did because learning had been ingrained in them for years. It was all new to me. Over the first two years, I learned to study: to memorize, take good notes, synthesize concepts, and recall all that I'd studied. During those years, I spent a lot of time in the library studying, and I developed a reputation as a pretty boring guy. But after those years, I'd learned the fine art of studying, and some of my classmates asked me to teach them how. It was astounding to pay forward what I'd learned.

After a few years, my study strategies were finely honed. When I started college, I spent weeks writing and rewriting papers, but later, I developed the ability to read reams of papers and many books to prepare for a paper, and I could keep the ideas in my head and arrange them so that I could write papers in one pass. I wrote them four days before they were due to avoid any stress. If I spent too much time on them, my old fears would resurface, so this strategy worked well for me. My first draft was my last draft. I'd become a free man!

I've met with some gifted athletes who aren't satisfied with their success. Other athletes get to a level of excellence and stop reaching. They've found their comfort zone, and it's good enough for them... but not the men and women who met with me. They weren't happy with being very good at their sport—they wanted to be exceptional. They were willing to try new techniques and push the boundaries of physical fitness so they could perform at a higher level. Their passion for greatness propelled them to take more risks, so they failed more than other athletes, but that didn't bother them at all. They saw real progress, and each positive experience added a new neural pathway that confirmed their commitment. My message to them sounded like this: "You and your teammates and opponents are very talented. For you to be better than them, you have to use your talent in a different way." The owner of the Calgary Flames once told me:

> *Wayne, I have a lot of gifted athletes, but I look for those who have what you talk about: a thriving mindset, a never-good-enough attitude, always reaching for more. I want my players to listen to the coach and try something different. I don't want our players to just be exceptional athletes. I want them to adapt and*

thrive under pressure. It's not enough to follow a game plan. They need to think on their feet, find creative solutions, and create the magnificent moments we love to remember.

BECOMING A CANDIDATE FOR INSPIRATION

Are you ready to move forward, look for new opportunities, and take a bold step or two? If you've read this far, I assume you are! Let me offer a few concrete applications:

1) Identify your need for inspiration: Do you...

   ... Lean toward safety and stability? What's the payoff?

   ... Avoid challenges and corrective feedback?

   ... Feel threatened by others who are courageous and take risks?

   ... Achieve less than you could?

   ... Give up quickly when you feel that you're in over your head?

   ... Become frustrated and hesitant when someone invites you to try something new?

2) Engage with the person who believes in you: Will you...

   ... Share your hopes and fears with this person?

   ... Discuss the nature of your comfort zone and why it's appealing to you?

   ... Muster the first flickers of faith that taking a risk might be productive?

...Talk about how your strengths can make a difference as you take these steps?

...Receive the encouragement and affirmation that you can do it?

3) Take the steps: Will you...

...Visualize what success will look like?

...Prepare without being paralyzed by over-analysis?

...Take the first step, and then the next one?

...Reflect on what happened with the person you trust?

...See whatever happened, success or failure, as a learning experience?

...Repeat this process?

If you'll trust the person who believes in you and receive inspiration and affirmation with a believing heart, you'll take steps into a world of opportunities you've avoided before. Each step is significant. Each one reinforces a pattern of courageous action. You'll begin to see yourself as a competent person who isn't afraid to experiment and try something new. You'll be on your way to a flourishing life.

INSPIRING OTHERS

When we feel secure, develop the habit of moving out of our comfort zones, and see risks as a normal part of life, we'll inspire those around us. Inspiration, though, isn't high control. We need to let people own their journeys. Many parents are far too protective, preventing their children from learning from their mistakes. For instance, I've noticed a one-year-old take a couple of steps and fall, and the parents (usually just one of them) rush over to pick the baby up. It's more instructive for the child for the parents to wait thirty seconds or so to see if the child can get up again on his own. Of course, if the child has gotten hurt, that's different, but I'm talking about the normal behavior of babies who are learning to walk. Smothering them with attention and rescuing them from every discomfort takes initiative from them, and worse, it communicates that the child can't make it on his own. "Helicopter parents" have raised a generation of kids who haven't learned how to take risks and learn from success and failure. Playgrounds today have spongy floors so kids who fall don't get hurt. What does this say to them? When I was a boy, my friends and I climbed trees, and we had to determine if a limb could hold us. We fell enough times to be a good judge of the strength of the limbs! We learned to use critical thinking and discovery to keep from breaking an arm or a leg in a fall (or at least, from breaking it again).

Parents who are too involved assume they're just being outstanding parents, but they're causing far more harm than they realize. When parents protect too much and take away opportunities to learn from successes and mistakes, kids don't develop adequate decision-making skills. Psychologist Jeff Gardere observes, "When we give children a space to be able to explore who they are, to be able to fall down, sometimes to be able to make mistakes, if they're not too big a mistake, that they tend to learn much more from those particular situations than they may from parents who may want to be able to tell the child what to do or, you know, is hovering over the child all the time." The mental health effects are alarming. Children who are smothered with protection and direction have increased levels of depression, anxiety, self-harm, and suicide.[19]

The same kind of smothering authority is often found in the business world. Bosses give detailed job descriptions and rigid schedules to employees, and they demand complete compliance. That kind of management may be appropriate if you're making a spacecraft or an atomic bomb, but in most offices, wise leaders share their vision and invite employees to find creative ways to get the job done. The boss cares very much about excellence, but he takes a different route to get there, one that shows that he values the people on the team and invites them to bring their best to work each day. Each affirmation of a skill employed and a job well done strengthens the relational bond and adds to the employees' sense of purpose. That's how a healthy corporate culture is formed and reinforced. That's the kind of company people want to work for.

In a *Forbes* article on how to create a positive environment at work, Caroline Castrillon recommends:

Research shows that employees are motivated to do their best when they feel appreciated. Not only that, but gratitude at work creates a domino effect within the organization. Showing appreciation towards

---

[19] Teresa Priolo, "Helicopter parenting: Study shows negative effects on kids' development," *Fox 5 New York*, 29 March, 2023, https://www.fox5ny.com/news/helicopter-parenting-study-negative-effects-on-kids-development.

> *someone will likely inspire them to "pay it forward" and thank others. . . . Public shout-outs are another effective recognition technique. That's because acknowledging your teammates in a public forum inspires and motivates people while rewarding specific team members for a job well done. . . . If you get an email that seems blunt or aggressive, don't assume the person is that way intentionally. Try to give them the benefit of the doubt by thinking the best instead of expecting the worst. . . . Positive thinking at work helps decision-making, facilitates interaction and increases resiliency. While it doesn't guarantee that everything will go your way, it will help put obstacles into perspective.[20]*

Affirmation is the indispensable sibling of inspiration. When we see people take a risk, even if they fail, we can say, "I'm so glad you gave that a try. Do it again. I'm sure you learned something from that attempt." And when we see one of our children do something kind, generous, or noble, we can affirm, "I saw that. That's what we value in our family, and that's what you showed. Way to go!"

---

20 Caroline Castrillon, "How to Embrace Positive Thinking at Work," *Forbes*, 23 June, 2022, https://www.forbes.com/sites/carolinecastrillon/2022/06/23/how-to-embrace-positive-thinking-at-work/?sh=2e64813c43b6.

Think about it:
1) What are some reasons it's important to trust someone and feel valued so you can receive that person's inspiring messages? What happens to those messages if we don't trust the person?
2) How would you describe the reasons connecting and inspiring are the cornerstones of growth?
3) As you've read this chapter, what opportunities have come to mind, maybe those you missed in the past?
4) What are the fears that keep people imprisoned in passivity? How did the fears rob them of initiative?
5) Answer the questions under "Becoming a Candidate for Inspiration."
6) What are the steps you want and need to take?
7) How will you prepare to take them?
8) When and how will you take them?
9) How will you process your experiences?

CHAPTER

7

Build

True success is achieved by harnessing the power of your strengths to step outside your comfort zone, where growth and opportunities await.
—Unknown

When I worked alongside master masons, I was impatient with their meticulous efforts to get the cornerstones exactly right, but when they were finally satisfied, building the walls proceeded very quickly. Each concrete block or brick was inserted with care, with plumb lines and horizontal strings marking each row. I may have been standing around while they positioned the cornerstone just right, but no longer. I mixed mortar, hauled bricks, and built scaffolding when the walls rose above head high.

That's a picture of the third phase of transformation: Connecting and inspiring are the cornerstones of a good foundation, and now we can build with visible, measurable, and encouraging progress. It doesn't take long for us to need good scaffolding—in the form of workable strategies to use our strengths to their full effect—so we can build higher. For us, each brick we put in place (that is, each choice to take a risk and try something new) makes small changes in our brain wiring, and the cumulative effect, just like creating a wall brick after brick, is both obvious and dramatic.

Without the foundation of feeling valued and inspired, people are naturally afraid to take risks, but with that bedrock confidence, they lay courses of bricks by learning—then doing—being encouraged and learning—and doing again—being encouraged and learning—and doing again—and on and on.

This doesn't mean that every risk taken will be wildly successful, but when we feel safe and valued, failure becomes a valuable learning experience instead of a disaster for our self-esteem. We no longer turn inward and defensive, or quickly point the finger of blame at others, when things don't go the way we planned. We take time to reflect on what went right and what went wrong, we welcome the feedback of others, especially those who have believed in us all along, and we learn so we can try again with the hope of better results. The safe person or encouraging social network (if we've found more than one person who values us), isn't surprised when we hit a rough patch and doesn't scowl when we fail. To use a different metaphor, when a football team is behind by two points and the last seconds of the game are ticking off, the coach is more supportive, more encouraging, and more intensely hopeful his quarterback will be able to make a play to win the game. That's the kind of "coach" each of us needs.

We need both validation and affirmation. They certainly overlap, but they're distinct. Validation is about who you are; affirmation is about what you do. We validate a spouse when we give and receive affection and say, "I'm so glad I married you!" We affirm a spouse when we say, "Wow, you did that so well," or "How did you think to do it that way?" A dad made a commitment to speak specifically to each of his two high school kids, "I love you, and I'm so proud of you," and "Hey, you're really good at..." He related, "You should see their faces when I say this to them. They beam! I want to say it often enough that it really sinks in, but not so often that they think I'm just saying it." He seems to be striking the right balance. At work, validation sounds like, "I'm glad you're on the team. You add so much!" And affirmation is more specific: "When you did that, it was the key to our success with that project. Way to go!"

> It's not enough to just say, "Good job." People need more than that.

Think about the times when someone spoke like this to you. It made a difference, didn't it? In his book, *Advice My Parents Gave*

Me: And Other Lessons I Learned from My Mistakes, Rodolfo Costa recalls this message from his parents: "Cultivate an optimistic mind, use your imagination, always consider alternatives, and dare to believe that you can make possible what others think is impossible."[21] All of us need to hear encouragement like this, and all of us need to give it.

It's not enough to just say, "Good job." People need more than that. They need someone to stop, reflect, and point out their specific contributions. Too often, parents, grandparents, supervisors, and spiritual leaders praise a person's intellect or the outcome of their efforts. Paradoxically, this can create the fear of being "not as smart as" someone else and a reluctance to take risks because the outcome isn't guaranteed. It's better to praise people for their efforts in the process, which affirms their willingness to try something new, even if it doesn't work out. Carol Dweck observes:

- People praised for their effort welcome challenging tasks, but those praised for their intelligence choose the easy route to guarantee success.
- People praised for effort worked longer and harder and enjoyed it more, but those praised for their intelligence gave up more easily.
- People praised for their effort demonstrated improved performance, but those praised for their intelligence showed less improvement.[22]

---

21 Rodolfo Costa, *Advice My Parents Gave Me: And Other Lessons I Learned from My Mistakes* (self-published, 2022).

22 Adapted from "The Not So Good about 'Good Job,'" *Bearfoot Occupational Therapy*, 10 June 2021, https://www.bearfootoccupationaltherapy.com/post/the-not-so-good-about-good-job.

Specific affirmation about effort and process shows people how their actions align with the larger purpose . . . of the family, the business, the team, or the church. When they connect these dots, they'll almost certainly repeat their actions, sharpen them, and feel more encouraged that they're having an impact on others.

THE POWER OF SMALL WINS

Harvard professor Teresa Amabile and psychologist Steven Kramer developed "The Progress Principle," which asserts that our experience of small wins has the same impact as big ones: it gives us confidence, renews our energy, and propels our hope for a win the next time we take a risk. They explain that every step forward releases dopamine and activates the brain's reward circuits. We experience a profound sense of satisfaction, and we want to do it again and again.[23]

Virtually all amazing inventions and discoveries are the result of many, sometimes seemingly countless, steps of trial and error. For instance:

- When he was twenty-two, Walt Disney was fired from a job at a newspaper because he "lacked imagination and had no good ideas." But he didn't stop trying. In fact, in the years after he started his own company, he and his team produced some of the most advanced technologies in cinema.

---

23 Teresa Amabile and Steven Kramer, *The Progress Principle: Using Small Wins to Ignite Joy, Engagement, and Creativity at Work* (Cambridge, MA: Harvard Business Review Press, 2011).

- Alexander Graham Bell struggled for a decade to win acceptance of his invention, the telephone. For him, the challenge wasn't in the creation but in the defense of his ownership of the idea. He endured years of legal conflicts over his patent.
- We know Henry Ford developed the assembly line to produce his radical invention of the first mass-produced car, but that wasn't his first attempt. A few years earlier, he launched the Detroit Automobile Company, which soon went bankrupt.
- Robert Goddard's design for liquid-fueled rockets was a source of ridicule in the scientific community, but his concepts were the foundation of the space program.
- Albert Einstein failed the entrance exam to get into college. He finally got in, but he then had difficulty deciding between a career selling insurance or working at the patent office. The office job gave him time to think, which proved to be more profitable than anyone could have imagined.
- William and Orville Wright owned a bicycle shop, but they had dreams of finding a way to fly. They built several prototypes, all of which crashed, until that windy day on an island off the coast of North Carolina in 1903 when their airplane flew for ten seconds . . . and the age of aviation was born.
- Virtually every one of Steve Jobs' innovations in technology was brilliant but initially flawed. Still, he put them on the market and ironed out the bumps on the run. He was an

irascible person who was kicked out of his own company after one too many spats with the board of directors.

When we read the synopses of the lives of these creative people, we seldom get to look behind the scenes at the countless small wins required to create what appeared to be a sudden and stunning success. They laid brick after brick, inspired by every small win, and eventually, they saw astounding things happen. Bell observed, "The most successful men, in the end, are those whose success is the result of steady accretion."[24] The point is that they never stopped learning, never stopped trying, and never stopped believing the solution would appear.

NEW SKILLS

As the scaffolding goes higher and we see progress, we're also more aware of potential problems. In masonry, each floor higher requires more care to keep bricks from falling on the people below—people like me! As we notice these challenges, we develop new skills to meet them. I play a little golf. I love to swing hard to drive the ball from the tee, but if I haven't developed the ability to hit a sand wedge, I might flail away in a trap and take many strokes to get out. I don't have to be an expert with a sand wedge, but I need to be at least proficient enough to get the ball on the green from the traps.

---

[24] Donovan Alexander, "9 Influential Inventors Who Failed Multiple Times Before Reaching Success," *Interesting Engineering*, 28 July, 2021, https://interestingengineering.com/lists/9-influential-inventors-who-failed-multiple-times-before-reaching-success.

> **Success seldom happens for the proverbial Lone Ranger; it happens far more often as a collective, collaborative effort.**

In all aspects of my life, I need to sharpen my skills, but I also need to be aware of my limitations. I can mitigate some of those limitations by developing them into strengths, or at least adequacies (like using a sand wedge), or I can find someone to come alongside and use his or her strengths to solve my problem. Success seldom happens for the proverbial Lone Ranger; it happens far more often as a collective, collaborative effort. Learning and growing together is more effective, and too, it's a lot more fun. In this environment, those who might be only surviving or protecting get a picture of what life can be, and they have the incredible benefit of being surrounded by others who care for them and see potential in them.

NAGGING FEARS

As I've met with men and women in the building phase, I've seen that their fears haven't suddenly vanished. Yes, they have supportive, encouraging relationships; yes, their vision for their lives is clearer and stronger than ever, yes, they're seeing real success as they step out in faith; and yes, they're learning valuable lessons from success and failure . . . but the fear is still lurking behind all this progress.

Some have catastrophized for so many years that any hint of failure sends them down a rabbit hole of self-doubt. They assume the worst, they magnify the obstacles, and they remember times when failure crushed their sense of significance. As they look at the present challenge, they see only the worst possible outcome. There are many ways to address this inordinate but very real fear, including sharing openly with someone who cares and understands, accepting uncertainty as a reality of life, journaling to clarify the situation and minimize the fear, and finding the courage to challenge the fear more than fearing the challenge.

Oddly, some people are afraid of success. It feels so unfamiliar because disappointment is their comfort zone where they've lived for a long time. They may be afraid they'll turn into someone they don't like, maybe like a successful, powerful person who has intimidated them in the past. They may be afraid they'll lose friendships if they move up the corporate ladder, and worse, former friends will become adversaries. But others may be afraid of success because they look beyond the immediate glory and doubt they can repeat it or sustain it. They're sure that success today will expose them to mockery when they fail tomorrow.

The building phase of transformational change focuses on identifying and developing strengths, but each success can surface latent fears. These, too, need to be identified so they can be addressed. If not, we can self-sabotage, doing things that result in failure, which reinforces the fear of taking a bold step in the future.

When I talk to people in this phase, I often ask simple questions to tap into their curiosity and imagination, such as,

"What if you succeed? What then?"

"What if you fail? How will you respond?"

"What are you learning from your experiences?"

"What about your efforts gives you pleasure?"

"What might be some fears that are holding you back?"

When people enter the building phase, they're like novice masons. They've watched the masters do their job, and they're ready to try their hand at it too. The first attempts are, to put it nicely, less than stellar, but if they keep practicing, their skills progress and they become increasingly proficient.

I think of this process as building on, building up, and building forward:

We *build on* when people who care about us help us identify our strengths. These may have been evident since we were kids, but in many cases, they've been hidden under our fear and passivity.

We *build up* when we apply our strengths to new opportunities. We experience small wins, and we're thrilled. We also experience some setbacks, and we learn from them.

We *build forward* when we walk through open doors of new applications for our strengths. We never dreamed of working with those outstanding people, taking on those important tasks, and having such significant responsibilities, but we've proven ourselves to those who are watching us, and they swing these doors open for us.

OVERCOMING

I've had the privilege to meet with some of the most courageous people on earth—people in the armed services who have lost a limb, eyesight, or mobility, but they've joined organizations to be with others who are making life work against long odds. They could have sunk deep into self-pity and resentment, but they've stepped into a world of new possibilities, reaching forward, finding solutions, and encouraging each other every step of the journey. Their attitude is: "Life hasn't turned out the way I planned, but I'm putting the pieces together in a way that offers a future of hope, fulfillment, and effectiveness." When the full impact of their loss became evident, they may have had a surviving mindset, but they've moved through the stages to a thriving mindset.

In an extraordinary plot twist, Steven Elliott joined the U.S. Army after the attacks on 9/11 and was assigned to the same Ranger platoon as former NFL star Pat Tillman. On April 22, 2004, friendly fire during an ambush took Tillman's life. Elliott was told by a wounded soldier that he may have fired the round that killed Tillman. Elliott had always believed in God, hard work, and serving his country, and he was devastated by his mistake. In his memoir, he describes how he lost his faith and spiraled "into the depths of guilt, shame and addiction." In early 2018 as he worked on his book, the publisher asked him to make some changes in the manuscript. He found a quiet place in the basement of a coffee shop. As he worked in the darkness of the basement and the darkness of his heart, an elderly man limped down the steps to wipe off the tables. The man asked Elliott if he could talk to him about Jesus, and a torrent of emotion spilled out of him. Later, he commented that his book "does not exist if not for a disabled Vietnam vet sitting down preaching the gospel to me." His website features a prominent sentiment: "Sometimes the real fight starts after the battle."[25] For Elliott, it took the compassion and initiative of a wounded warrior to turn his life around.

When Sarah got married, she told her husband Beau that she wasn't interested in having children. Beau thought she'd come around, but after a couple of years, Sarah was even more adamant that she didn't want kids. He tried to probe gently several times, but she deflected the conversation to other topics. Finally, he waded in: "I know you don't want to talk about this, but it's important—to both of us. What's the story of you not wanting children?"

The moment must have been right because instead of getting angry and shutting down, she wept as she told Beau about the chaos and abuse she'd experienced as a child. In grim detail, she described yelling, hitting, and being locked in her room by her mother—not to protect her from the fury between her parents, but to prevent her from intervening to help them resolve their fierce argument. "I was just trying to help," she wept. Beau and

---

25 Randy Gonzales, "Soldier found hope for 'War Story,'" *The Hayes Daily News*, November 29, 2019.

Sarah talked about her childhood many times over the next few months, and it didn't take him long to understand her reluctance: She didn't want to treat her own children the way she'd been treated. Her solution was simple: She refused to have kids.

The next six months were both excruciatingly hard and deeply healing for Sarah. She realized she had strengths her parents (especially her mother) had never displayed. Beau gave her plenty of room to grieve, think, and imagine being a good mother someday. He never pushed; he just let her know he understood. One day Sarah announced to Beau that she wasn't going to take birth control pills any longer. She told him she was still afraid, but she was counting on him to help her show love instead of cruelty to their child. A few months later, she got pregnant.

For six or seven months after their baby Caroline was born, Sarah had some flashbacks and fear flooded her heart, but gradually, Beau's confidence and kindness began to melt the fear away. Sarah's friends remarked that she was a terrific mother ... only Beau and her two or three closest friends knew the story of her journey from paralyzing fear to quiet confidence. Today, she and Beau have four lovely children, and yes, Sarah is a terrific mom. She is attentive without being overbearing, loving without smothering, and sparking a world of creativity in her kids instead of the terror she suffered when she was their age. Sarah had moved from surviving as a child to protecting as a young adult, to a builder with a very high scaffold as a young mom.

Abraham Lincoln is known as one of the best presidents in the history of the United States, but many people don't know the backstory. He grew up in abject poverty under the harsh hand of his demanding father. He had almost no formal education, but he learned to read and devoured every book he could get his hands on. Two women who meant the most to him, his stepmother and his girlfriend, died, and the loss was almost more than he could bear. A friend took away his razor, knife, and scissors because he was afraid Lincoln would use them on himself.

Later, he married Mary Todd, a woman almost the polar opposite of his personality. Tragically, two of their sons died in childhood, one in Springfield, Illinois, where Lincoln was a lawyer, and the other during his time in the White House. He was a remarkable leader of a war-time government, but he was even more remarkable as a human being. One historian cites Lincoln's compassion when he pardoned a deserter who left his post because his family was destitute. The writer explains:

> *Lincoln's compassion and mercy are central to his legacy, and the picture that has come down to us envisions him as a man who was generous of spirit, who pardoned soldiers who fell asleep on guard duty, showed leniency whenever possible, even to deserters, and aided widows and orphans. Because of his position as President, he had opportunities to prove or disprove this reputation, as many requests for pardons, deferrals of executions, and pleas to aid soldiers came to him.*[26]

---

[26] "The Compassion and Mercy of President Abraham Lincoln," *RAAB Collection*, https://www.raabcollection.com/presidential-autographs/lincoln-pardon-1863.

In his second inaugural address, delivered only weeks before he was assassinated, Lincoln shared his vision of a better future when the war ended:

With malice toward none; with charity for all; with firmness in the right, as God gives us to see the right, let us strive on to finish the work we are in; to bind up the nation's wounds; to care for him who shall have borne the battle, and for his widow, and his orphan—to do all which may achieve and cherish a just, and a lasting peace, among ourselves, and with all nations.

Lincoln went through very dark periods of his life when surviving was the best he could do, but he learned valuable lessons that kindness, humility, wisdom, and strength could coexist in one person. He learned to thrive.

I work with a local organization that is implementing our flourishing model as they help disadvantaged students in the school system. Some of them have dropped out of school and are living on the street, and they have frequent interactions with the justice system. The organization's leaders asked me to come to their offices to make a short video presentation, and there, I met a young woman who impressed me. After we talked for a few minutes, I asked her, "What's your story?"

She smiled and replied, "I used to be a client of the program, and my coach saw potential in me—potential I'd never seen in myself." The organization enlists business executives to coach students for an extended time, often two to three years. She had been "a mess" when she entered the program, but after a while, the leaders noticed her exemplary character and organizational talents, so they hired her. She explained, "I bought into what the program offered me, and I've made progress. I'm not a mess anymore." Without a hint of arrogance, she told me, "Dr. Hammond, I've earned the right to be here."

Only a couple of years before, she had been barely surviving on the street, but a coach connected with her to give her the safety she never had and the value she longed for, inspired her to think what her life could become, and built a new life brick by brick. She was thriving now. I had planned for the video to be about our model of transformation, and the person standing in front of me was a prime example.

The leader of the organization told me, "We view everyone as an amazing person, with untapped and unlimited potential. We don't see these young people as problems; we see an amazing future for each of them."

A foundation of connecting and inspiring is essential for us to utilize our strengths in constructive ways in the building phase. Otherwise, we use them to manipulate people, and they feel used; we compete in unhealthy ways with them, so they feel angry; or we hide from them, so they feel unwanted. Each phase of transformation is rooted in relationships.

Think about it:
1) Can you recall a time when someone was intensely for you, like a football coach cheering his quarterback on at a

crucial point in a game? If so, how did it make you feel? If not, what do you think you've missed?
2) Describe the difference in the impact of being praised for your effort and your tenacity to stay in the process instead of your intelligence and skill.
3) What can you say to a family member or teammate besides, "Good job"?
4) What difference will it make?
5) What has to happen in your mind for this change to become a habit?
6) How do small wins (and good lessons from failures) affect our brains?
7) Review the section on nagging fears and answer the questions.
8) Which of the stories about overcoming is most meaningful to you? Explain your answer.

CHAPTER 8

Empower

Start by doing what is necessary, then what is possible, and suddenly you are doing the impossible.
—quote by Saint Francis of Assisi

People who feel empowered are fully present in the moment—their confidence has overcome any tendency to manipulate or dominate people out of fear. In their process of growth, they've developed the ability to adapt to new situations. They expect new challenges and embrace them as fresh opportunities to learn and grow. This is more than acquiring a set of valuable skills; it's the wisdom to apply those skills in an ever-expanding set of circumstances. The combination of confidence, competence, and wisdom enables them to be calm and effective in almost all situations.

In chapter 1, I related the story of Bethany, a girl who at the time should have been a carefree student in high school but was an addict and a prostitute who had already had three abortions. If there was a picture of a seemingly hopeless plight, she was it. But Marcia, her caseworker, loved her and believed in her. As you may recall, I met Bethany at an awards ceremony, and I was in awe of her courage and wisdom. She invited me to her college graduation, and there, my amazement deepened even more. Today, she is paying it forward by pouring into other young women whose lives have gone off the rails. Because of Marcia, Bethany learned to live with a beautiful blend of courage and humility. She still has memories of the trauma she suffered, some inflicted by others and some at her own hands, but those thoughts no longer define and dominate her. Bethany is defined by her personal strengths, her environmental strengths, and her performance strengths. She's living her aspiration to make a difference in the lives of young women who feel utterly helpless and hopeless. She is, I don't think it's too much to say, a new person. I'm grateful to have gotten a glimpse of her flourishing, effective, richly colored life. She is empowered with the quiet inner strength to engage others with genuine care that's unencumbered by the urge to please people to win approval, dominate them to always be one up, or hide from uncomfortable moments of tension. She has a broad repertoire of proven skills, strengths, and support, so she knows that she can handle whatever life throws at her. She can navigate rough waters in ways that are meaningful to her and bring her success.

> People who are empowered value people very highly, but they're no longer dependent on them for every decision.

The stages of surviving and protecting are dominated by the past, so people are understandably defensive. When we enter the striving phase, the chains of the past are unlocked, and a new world of possibilities opens to us . . . but we're still acquiring the strengths we'll need to flourish. Now, in the thriving stage, we're putting all we've learned into action. Instead of being defensive or unsure, we're gaining self-confidence so our gaze can be upward and outward. A critical component in this stage is the desire and the ability to create an exponential impact that's far greater than our limited efforts. We now collaborate gladly and effectively.

People who are empowered value people very highly, but they're no longer dependent on them for every decision. Because they've been affirmed and encouraged, they've developed inner strength, so they become autonomous, proactive learners who take smart risks in ways that maximize their ongoing success. Only people who feel safe and valued can be confident in their unique capacities to learn, and they eagerly embrace new ideas and strategies to experience "what might be" instead of settling for stultifying safety. Each success broadens and deepens the foundation of confidence to be more and do more. Gradually, they acquire and apply growth-oriented strategies, taking more smart risks, expanding their impact, and growing in their sense of competency.

I overheard a conversation between two young people who recently entered the work world. One of them told the other, "I've got some big decisions to make. I need you to stay with me, give me your advice, and hold me accountable. I don't know what I'd do without you."

The other one replied, "Yeah, I've got some big ones too, but I've listened to my mentor and made my decision. I think it's a good direction for me."

Do you see the difference? The first person expressed dependence and a lack of confidence, but the other one displayed an inner sense of empowerment—seeking input but making an autonomous decision. The second person owned the process of discovery as well as the decision.

Let me identify and explain several common traits of people who are empowered:

1) They're curious.

I've noticed something about myself: The more I learn, the less I realize I know. Each new insight opens more doors of discovery. I may have acquired a lot of ideas throughout my life, but I have so much more to learn. Empowered people are naturally curious. They ask a lot of questions to probe, explore, and understand. I enjoy teaching first-year psychology students. They know just enough to be dangerous, but they're eager to learn.

Like every aspect of being empowered, curiosity becomes an intuitive trait, and we're never content to rest on what we already know. This is the adventure of continuous learning.

2) They're humble.

Proud people are sure they're always right, but empowered people recognize there are usually several different ways to look at any situation. Knowledge isn't the same as wisdom. Smart people may spout off what they know to impress others, but wise people ask questions to understand people better. Years ago, an elder of a tribe of indigenous people heard me speak, and when I'd finished, he took me aside and said, "Wayne, God gave you two eyes, two ears, but one mouth. What do you think he was trying to say to you?" I got the message . . . loud and clear.

Insecure people either talk too much or not at all. Those who talk too much are trying to impress, to prove they're okay. Those who remain almost mute have given up on impressing anyone; they just don't want to look foolish and become the target of ridicule. When I'm around people who ask more questions than making declarations, I assume there's more to them than meets the eye.

3) They're bold.

But without being obnoxious! Perpetual boldness isn't a strength. It's a sign the person feels very uncomfortable with ambiguity and is covering up insecurity with bravado. Empowered people know the difference between convictions, opinions, and ideas. They can stand strong on their convictions and let others feel free to disagree with their ideas and opinions. A different perspective doesn't necessarily mean one is right and the other is a fool, but that attitude has become common in our discourse today. Author Simon Sinek observes:

> *When we vehemently disagree with people we've never met, we can start to dehumanize them. See them as evil. The only way we can ever advance as a society is when we learn to see each other as humans. Complex, messy humans. That's why we need Robin Steinberg's message! She understands compassion in a way few others do. As a career public defender and criminal justice reformer, she had to learn to see the humanity in people, even if they may have done horrible things.*[27]

What's the hill you're willing to die on? If it's everything, you're going to die a thousand relational deaths and alienate people who could have been friends. You may impress a few people with your fire, but you'll burn others who no longer want to be around you.

Those who enjoy inner security are less judgmental. If I believe that every person has a bit of the image of God in them, and therefore they have inestimable value, I will respect them even if I strongly disagree with their perspective about an issue. When I meet with someone who is fiercely defensive or, on the other end of the spectrum, painfully withdrawn, I make the assumption that he or she has suffered terribly in the past, and these behaviors are their best ways to try to cope with the immense heartache. I don't

---

[27] Simon Sinek, *LinkedIn* post, https://www.linkedin.com/posts/simonsinek_when-we-vehemently-disagree-with-people-we-activity-7044385149349687296-ML_A.

despise the ones who bluster, and I don't ignore the ones who are trying their best to remain invisible. All of them are valuable in God's sight, and if I see them through His eyes, I'll see them that way in mine too.

> Risk-taking isn't a blind leap into the dark. It's a carefully considered decision based on a backlog of positive experiences.

If we want insecure people to grow up emotionally, we need to realize it does no good to either blame them or try to instruct them out of their condition. To become confident, wise, humble people, they need to feel understood and known, safe and secure, so their defenses can be replaced with confidence and competence.

Empowerment is a learned trait. We acquire it by starting wherever we are on the continuum and moving from surviving to protecting to building to empowering. It's much more than gaining a wealth of information, and in fact, in the earlier stages, information is often used as a weapon to dominate or impress. Courage, then, is a trait that's developed as a new habit as we become increasingly secure and confident in our abilities.

Risk-taking isn't a blind leap into the dark. It's a carefully considered decision based on a backlog of positive experiences.

4) They live with a blend of purpose and passion.

When I encounter empowered people, I invariably notice a spark—a flash of passion, of almost insatiable desire to make a difference. I met a man who, after getting his law degree, joined a firm and received a starting salary of $250,000 a year. But the work and the money weren't fulfilling to him. He met someone who worked for an organization caring for underprivileged kids, and the spark ignited a flame in him. He left his law practice and joined the staff of the nonprofit organization. He told me, "Wayne, needless to say, I took a cut in pay, but I got a huge raise in fulfillment. At the law firm, I was competent, but it felt kind of empty. Here, I've been able to align my competence with my passion. It makes all the difference."

On a trip to New Zealand, I met a high school girl and her dad. She started a movement of collecting plastic items along shorelines to rid the oceans of this pollutant that causes the deaths of wildlife. When I saw her speak on stage, I was very impressed with her boldness and passion, and then, when I met her father, I realized she had gotten her strength from him. He didn't give her the vision, and he didn't try to control it, but he supported her every step of the way. He helped her use videos and other technologies to communicate her message and recruit people to the cause. Over time, her sense of empowerment will grow and mature, but she's off to an impressive start!

I've had the privilege to work with some gang leaders in Toronto. It has been an honor to watch corporate executives mentor them. These young men are leaders because they've taken control of people, products, and an area of the city. They feel empowered because they've gained a lot of power, largely through intimidation. For them to change, they have to see that something else is more important and more valuable. The executives shared their stories of being entrepreneurs—their successful ventures and their failures. Conversations went something like this:

The executive tells his story, and then asks, "Tell me. How much money did you make last year?"

Gang leader: "Half a mil."

Exec: "Impressive, but that comes with the risk of being arrested and doing time. I've noticed something about you: You're very organized, you plan well, and you delegate responsibility. You have refined leadership skills. I look for these qualities in people I hire. By the way, I made $3 million last year, and there isn't a cell door in my future. Would you like to learn how to make that much?"

Gang leader: "Yeah, that sounds pretty good, but I don't know. Maybe it's not right for me."

Exec: "Sure, you'd have to learn to apply your talents in a different environment, but from what I've seen, that won't be a problem. Are you interested?"

These business leaders didn't write the gang leaders off (like most of us do). They took the time to engage with them, share their stories, accentuate strengths, and give them a vision of a better life. The relationship broke down barriers on both sides, leading to a more flourishing life for both. The connection wasn't over when the gang leader accepted the invitation. It was just beginning. The executive continued to mentor the gang leader through the process of growth and change. This was a classic example of connect and inspire, which then led to a process to refine existing competencies and uncover new ones, which led to the former gang leader being empowered to live a more productive, meaningful life ... without living under the constant threat of doing ten to twenty years in prison.

This wasn't just an idea, and it wasn't merely an academic theory. Two of the gang leaders went through the entire process and became very successful entrepreneurs.

POWER VS. EMPOWERED

When many of us think of someone with power, we imagine (or more likely, we remember) someone who has taken a one-up position, insisting on having the first and last word in any discussion, and who never admits defeat. We see images of people who can't be happy unless they make others feel *less than*. Some go so far as positioning themselves in "the dragon seat" in meetings so nothing can happen behind them, and they are the center of attention in the room. But this is the opposite of true empowerment!

People who are empowered have strength tempered with kindness, understanding, and wisdom. They treat others with respect, and the response is predictable: others want to join them in fulfilling their vision. Apple founder Steve Jobs was a complicated person, but he could inspire enormous creativity in the people around him. He believed in them, and they knew it. They brought their best to the company every day, and Apple created some of the most remarkable products of our age. Jobs was a master at attracting highly competent and creative people and then empowering them to unleash their potential. Many of us bought Apple products at the beginning simply because the company was cool, but we now buy them because they're so easy to use.

Those who feel empowered don't demand compliance; they inspire collaboration. Empowered people empower others.

Pride can look strong on the surface, but it's based in a deep-rooted insecurity. It's the fear of losing control and the demand to be in control. Jesus tells us that to have the ultimate sense of identity, we need to let go of an inferior one. We trade our flawed, self-absorbed agenda for God's far greater agenda. If we insist on being in control, we'll always be afraid of being out of control, but if our new identity as *a dearly beloved masterpiece in the eyes of God* takes root in our souls, our natural pride, fear, and shame will be melted by the limitless love of Jesus. Then we won't be tied up in knots trying to prove ourselves, we won't second guess everything we say or is said to us, and we won't be terrified of someone finding out the truth about us. The paradox is that when we're empty of self-defense and self-promotion, we're filled with the purpose, pleasure, and power of God. That's a pretty good swap if you ask me.

What does empowerment look like in a business setting? There are countless examples, but here's one: A supervisor might say to a staff member, "We're having a meeting on Monday morning to try to fix the screw-up that happened yesterday. You need to be there." The staff member will be afraid all weekend, wondering if she'll be blamed for the problem! But instead, in the same situation, an empowered supervisor might say, "As you know, we had a challenging situation this week. On Monday morning, we're going to talk about it and find a solution. I want you to be there because you always have great ideas about solving problems like this." The weekend for the staff member would be much different after hearing this message!

As I live in this fourth stage of being empowered, I have a deep sense of being content with who I am. I'm not trying to fool anyone, and I'm not ashamed of who I am. I can be curious and innovative without fear of things not going as well as I'd like. I can take risks and learn from whatever happens. But it's not just about me. My real joy is in the impact I can have on others, especially those who feel left behind or marginalized, like addicts, prostitutes, gang leaders, students, overworked teachers, and any others who are trying to hide their desperation. I want to be a part of something bigger—much bigger—than myself. I don't want to be an island; I want to be one part of a vast archipelago.

People who are empowered are wonderful spouses and parents, affirming business leaders, encouraging coaches, and terrific friends. They aren't spending their emotional energy on image management, so they can give themselves freely and gladly to those around them. Don't you want to be that kind of person?

Think about it:

1) What are some traits a person may need to build before the empowerment stage?
2) Why is being curious a characteristic of someone who feels empowered?
3) What may have inhibited curiosity before?
4) What unleashes it now? And humility? Boldness?
5) I mentioned that some people have a certain "spark" of purpose and passion. Can someone have that spark in the stages of surviving and protecting? Why or why not?
6) How about in the building stage?
7) What is most attractive to you about the description in this chapter of being empowered?
8) Do you have any sense of resistance? If so, describe it.

CHAPTER 9

The Journey

Courage is not the absence of fear, but the triumph over it. Embrace life's journey with resilience, grace, and competence, and you will conquer any obstacle in your path.
—quoted by Nelson Mandela

We live in an instant culture. From ancient times when the horse was domesticated until the advancing technology of steam engines on trains in the early 19th century, the fastest anyone could travel was the speed of a horse. (Some people thought that if a human body traveled any faster it would come apart!) Today, we not only travel at speeds that would have astounded observers only a few generations ago, we expect instantaneous results in drive-thru and online banking, picking up fast food, microwave cooking, and internet shopping... and we have instant access to an entire universe of information with only a few clicks on a keyboard.

It's no wonder, then, that many people are discouraged by the relatively slow process of personal change and growth. Expectations of immediate results make them (and me) impatient. In the spiritual realm, many believers who are wrestling with longstanding developmental issues think that if they pray that God will give them relief, they'll experience a "holy zap," and every problem will be fixed. Advanced technology is a wonderful modern tool, but we aren't AI robots. Human nature hasn't changed over countless millennia. We still need to acknowledge and embrace the process of change. Unrealistic expectations make us vulnerable to discouragement, so much so that we're tempted to quit moving forward. One person illustrated the process this way: "We may want to take a quick helicopter ride to the top of the mountain, but that's not the way life works. The hike up the mountain takes longer and requires more effort, but the views are spectacular! And besides, we're not hiking alone."

We take our first steps on this journey after years, and even decades, of walking in a different direction. To get on the right path and move forward, we need to understand the process. Alvin Toffler, the author of *Future Shock*, predicted, "The illiterate of the future are not those who can't read or write, but those who cannot learn, unlearn, and relearn."[28] Advancement, he asserts, requires us to *learn* new ideas and strategies, and at the same time, do the hard work to *unlearn* the entrenched patterns of thought and behavior we've relied on for years. As this transition

---

28 Alvin Toffler, *Future Shock* (New York, NY: Bantam, 1984).

is happening, we continually *relearn* new concepts and practices, refine them, improve them, and make them productive habits.

> When we sense that at least one person believes we're worth their investment of time and attention, our confidence grows.

This process involves insight and grace. We need insights about what was, what is, and what can be. Largely through interactions with a mentor, coach, or friend, our eyes are opened to new possibilities, and we have one or one hundred "Aha!" moments. Then, as we take the first halting steps and often fall on our faces because we've never walked this way before, we need grace—continuous regard and affirmation—from someone who believes in us and is patient with us on the journey. When we sense that at least one person believes we're worth their investment of time and attention, our confidence grows. Gradually, each lesson is applied in different contexts and situations, so our application of insights becomes more nimble. Our sense of identity evolves from fearful insecurity to stability to self-assurance. Then, the learning never ends, the application of insights continues, and we keep growing until our last days.

RESISTANCE

Perhaps the most pervasive reason people never start on this journey or give up too soon is multi-faceted fear: the fear of the unknown, the fear of failure, and the fear of rejection. These fears don't magically vanish; they must be eroded, sandpapered away by affirmation, small wins, and the courage to take the next step . . . and the next. Some days are better than others. On good days, we dig deep to find the courage to take the next bold step to speak up and apply what we've learned, but there are other days when our self-confidence has evaporated, perhaps from a misstep, and often from an unkind word from someone we respect (or maybe someone we don't respect but we've given power to their words). We may sit on the side of the path for a while, but sooner or later we stand up and take a step in the right direction.

Deeply ingrained feelings from past wounds and bad decisions can make even one step seem unimaginable. Unrelieved hurt, fear, anger, and shame are massive boulders on the path of change. We feel alone . . . helpless . . . hopeless, until someone connects with us, someone who knows the worst about us and loves us still. This relationship is a new foundation to craft a more wholesome identity. Then, we're open to new concepts and think better thoughts—we're inspired to dream again . . . or for the first time. We take the first steps of progress, and we slowly build a set of new skills. As we become more confident, we dare to explore, and we feel empowered to make a difference in the people around us. In case you missed it, each kind of resistance is overcome in the four stages of growth: connect, inspire, build, and empower.

A few of us are natural risk-takers, but the vast majority of us are hesitant. We overcome our resistance to change by *finding the courage* to take one more step out of our comfort zones, *exploring* a new way of living and relating, *reflecting* on what happened, and *applying* the lessons we learned from the experience. This is the template for embracing change. We may begin with borrowed hope, but practicing this sequence enough times gives us new convictions to live by.

Many of us are quite sensitive to criticism. Virtually any corrective comment, let alone a blast of condemnation, is a crushing blow. As the neuroplasticity of our brains changes through the growth process, we begin to interpret these events differently. Our amygdala isn't as easily triggered so we don't react as quickly, the sense of threat and doom gradually subside, and we become more objective. We have the inner strength to observe the other person without reacting defensively. We may discount the damage the person has intended because we recognize his desire to dominate through condemnation, so we don't take it personally, or we may value the person's criticism because we're strong enough to winnow the truth instead of being overcome by fear and shame. Even if someone is genuinely trying to hurt us, we can respond with wisdom and courage, remaining open to find even a kernel of truth in what was said. Increasing confidence enables us to reframe every encounter.

> **If we're waiting until our emotions are completely serene before we act, we'll never act.**

Of course, each step to learn, unlearn, and relearn requires enormous courage. Even when we're brave enough to take action, we may look confident on the outside, but until our brains are sufficiently rewired, we're shaking on the inside. But that's what it means to step out of our comfort zones! If we're waiting until our emotions are completely serene before we act, we'll never act.

A metaphor I've found helpful is to hold up a string, which represents the courage to face our fears and take action. One strand is fairly easy to break, but when several strands are woven together, the cumulative effect is that the rope is much harder to break. As we keep adding new strings of confidence and courage, it becomes something we can rely on when we encounter new and bigger challenges.

A group of people with very high levels of resistance to change are alcoholics and addicts. Their dependence on substances has a deep impact on every part of their lives: their daily habits, their cravings, their relationships, and the wiring of their brains. Groups like Alcoholics Anonymous and Narcotics Anonymous are successful when (and I'd argue only when) those who show up and admit their condition find support and accountability in a relationship with a sponsor. They may have felt alone before, but honest sharing in the group makes them feel understood, and the sponsor personalizes the honesty, support, and encouragement they need to keep walking through the steps.

In my experience with this population, the very best sponsors aren't those who simply tell people to avoid places and people who trigger their cravings. Instead, they take them to the last three steps where new, healthy habits become ingrained, neural wiring is changed, and the lessons learned in the group are applied in every aspect of their lives. The goal, then, is more than just being clean and sober; it's to restructure feelings, thoughts, and behavior so people genuinely flourish.

Sometimes well-meaning people try to scare alcoholics and addicts out of their self-destructive choices by saying, "If you keep this up, you're going to die!" That may be true, but few people are motivated by this threat. Those of us who want to help them need to identify deeper, better reasons to change, perhaps restoring a marriage or walking a daughter down the aisle at her wedding. Hope-based reasons to change are far more powerful than fear-based ones. Sponsors need to inspire people to dream new dreams.

FIRST, UNDERSTAND

In my observation, one of the primary reasons people choose to avoid the journey of growth is because they don't feel known. Those who have tried to help them jumped too quickly to solutions without taking the time to listen to their stories. In therapy sessions, when I sense the person is backing away and closing down, I say, "I don't think I've heard enough of your story. Would you tell me more about your background, your relationships, and how people and events have affected you?"

This is a common problem. Friends make assumptions about friends, spouses about spouses, and counselors about clients. Our intentions may be entirely benign, but we can leave people feeling half-known, half-understood, and half-loved. A few more questions and a little more time invite the person to share a little more, often uncovering parts of the story that are hidden from others, and often stored in a locked memory vault for many years.

It's not too much of a stretch to say that if people don't feel known and understood, the love, affirmation, and care expressed by others can feel relatively meaningless. The unspoken belief is, "They can't mean what they're saying because they don't really know me." Loneliness is an epidemic in our society today. We have more information about people than ever, but fewer people feel deeply known.

I see my primary role as a kind investigator, one who pursues the stories that have remained hidden, not to expose people to ridicule, but to take the threat of exposure away. The majority of people have never told their whole story to anyone, and even the bravest tell theirs in increments: A bit of vulnerability received with respect earns trust, so the next bit of honesty can be shared. Quite often when I understand someone more fully, they understand themselves better too. They see connections between events, people, feelings, thoughts, and behaviors that have existed for years but remained a mystery.

> **To be known but not loved is terrifying, but to be loved but not known is superficial and meaningless.**

We're naturally resistant to being fully known by anyone who hasn't proven to be safe. In fact, it's foolish to entrust our stories to untrustworthy people. To be known but not loved is terrifying, but to be loved but not known is superficial and meaningless. We need connections with people who know us well and don't run away, laugh at us, or condemn us . . . people who respect and value us with all our strengths and flaws.

Feeling understood—and feeling safe in being understood—is essential for emotional healing and personal growth. When I first felt deeply known, I was free in that relationship to be raw and real about my emotions, honest about my thoughts, and analytical about my behavior. Over the years, I've internalized what I've learned so I'm now a "curator of others' stories." It is my privilege to listen, to ask good questions, listen more, and connect the dots between past experiences and present desires.

When I realize I'm working harder than my client, I know I'm not on the right track. I've failed to tap into the deep recesses of their stories to uncover their strongest motivations. I need to slow down and listen. Instead of offering unsolicited advice, I need to ask questions like, "If you had those choices, which one would make the most sense to you?" After this discussion, I could ask, "How can I support you in this choice?" and then, "How will we know this path is making a difference in your life?" When the person has been inspired to take a significant step and comes back to see me, I ask for a report, and based on the reply, I respond with affirmation or a question: "From what you said you planned to do the last time we talked, it doesn't seem that it worked out. What's the disconnect? Tell me about it." It's my responsibility to find out what's meaningful to my client. If I've made wrong assumptions or I haven't taken enough time to listen, I'm wasting time for both of us.

If you haven't found someone who is both safe and interested in your story, don't stop until you find that person. As we've seen, one of our basic problems is that we often choose the wrong person. Someone seems nice, so we trust them, but that person may not have the training, personality, or capacity to listen without giving us simplistic solutions to our complex problems. It's discouraging to have our hopes dashed, especially if it happens two or three times. The journey of personal growth often includes some detours along the way. Don't be surprised if someone doesn't take the time to understand you and your story, but don't stop until you find someone who does.

This is the art of listening *to understand* instead of listening *to direct* . . . or listening *to correct.* Certainly, when our children are little, our parenting needs to be protective, but as they grow up, our role shifts from protecting to directing to influencing—and influencing is accomplished primarily through listening so we can help them interpret situations with wisdom and make increasingly better decisions. Our task isn't to control them before they leave home; it's to prepare them to be wise and confident well before they leave, with a proven track record of autonomy and growth. Our job isn't to protect them from bad choices; it's to invite them to examine their journey so they can learn from experience and internalize valuable lessons. If we're afraid of giving our sixteen-year-old the keys to the car because we don't believe she's ready, we've failed to give her experiences before that day so she can learn to drive.

> Don't be surprised if someone doesn't take the time to understand you and your story, but don't stop until you find someone who does.

In the same way, employers are often frustrated that the people who report to them don't take initiative, but the employers need to look in the mirror. They need to give their team members opportunities to learn and grow in a supportive environment where they get regular feedback. Then, when new challenges or opportunities arise, they're ready and eager to tackle them. They will take the initiative, own their decisions, and find creative ways to solve problems. (More on this in the chapter about work.)

When people feel understood and valued, they almost always find new ways to shine. We might believe that's an assumption we can make, but it isn't. Most people walk into my counseling office, the classroom, the office, or their living rooms with the opposite assumptions: *Nobody really knows me at the deepest level, and if they did, they wouldn't like me, love me, or want to be around me.* I make sure this message is clear when each client walks into my office. I say, "I want you to know that I value you for who you are, and what's important to you is important to me. I believe you're an amazing person with unlimited potential. You may just not know it yet. I'm here to help you on your journey. If I think a path you plan to take isn't wise, I'll tell you, but I'll support you as you make your own decision." That's not a bad message to communicate regularly to those who live under our roofs and work around us. Even if I disagree with what people believe is important, I still support their autonomy to make their own decisions.

SIGNS OF PROGRESS

Over the years, I've noticed some definitive patterns of behavior in people who are making real progress on their journey of growth, for instance:

1) I see it in their language.

   They're self-revealing without being defensive, and they interpret difficulties as opportunities instead of threats. They may have mumbled in the past because they were unsure of themselves, but now they speak clearly.

2) I see it in their demeanor.

   They may have shown signs of insecurity before, such as avoiding eye contact, but now they have more confidence. Self-assurance isn't arrogance; it's calm self-reliance that life isn't too much for them to handle. Brave people don't have to brag. They simply own their decisions.

3) I see it in their relationships.

   They no longer cower around strong people, and they no longer take advantage of weak people. They value each person and treat each one with respect. They can be honest without being cruel and kind without being overly sentimental.

4) I see it in their courage.

   They've developed the habit of reaching for more. They're thrilled with their successes, and they learn from their setbacks. Every new challenge is another step in the journey of growth. As their confidence grows, they don't ask what they should do. They're not dependent on others for their decisions. Instead, they describe the decision they made and what they learned from the experience. They own their decisions and the outcomes. They aren't devastated by failure. They take the time to reflect on what happened, and they're excited to apply the lessons they learned today to the opportunities of tomorrow.

The process of change may have seemed like a deep, dark unsolvable mystery in the past, but no longer. Some of the most joyful moments of my life occur when I see a smile on someone's face who has taken several steps on the journey and is thrilled with the progress. They were discouraged before, but now they're excited. They were weighed down by self-doubt before, but now their confidence is growing. A lady, I'll call her Jill, had suffered terrible abuse from her home environment and had replicated the pain in her marriage. In desperation, she joined a support group and soon found a wonderful sponsor. Gradually, the sponsor's love and acceptance began to break down thick walls of distrust. And gradually, Jill was able to share more details about her painful past. As she was increasingly vulnerable, her self-protective walls began to crumble, and Jill experienced love—by her admission, for the first time in her life. Later, at the beginning of a meeting, the leader noticed that Jill was beaming. He asked, "Okay, Jill, what's the deal? What happened to the Jill who used to be here?"

Jill laughed and cried at the same time. She couldn't contain her joy. "I just can't believe someone would love me ... really love *me*. It's too wonderful to even imagine, but it's true!"

She and her sponsor had traveled together on the journey. She still had a long way to go, but the progress she'd made so far was a thrill—for Jill, her sponsor, the group leader, and the rest of the group. Jill will never be the same.

Think about it:
1) How do you think the modern conveniences of an "instant society" have shaped your expectations of personal growth?
2) What is the combined impact on our journey of insight and grace? Why do we need both?
3) As you learn about this process of growth, what are some specific assumptions you need to unlearn? What difference will it make?
4) Why is it important to keep relearning the concepts of truth and grace?
5) How would you describe the importance of being understood? What happens when you feel deeply known and valued? What happens when you don't?
6) Which of the signs of progress are you seeing (or beginning to see) in yourself?
7) What's your next step on the journey?

CHAPTER 10

Flourishing at Home

Nurturing a culture of flourishing at home is like tending to a garden. With patience, love, and care, we can cultivate an environment where every member of the family can grow and thrive.
—Unknown

The message our spouse and children long to hear—and more than that, to *feel* deep in their bones—is, "You're a treasure to me. I accept you for who you are right now. I know you're on an adventure of learning, experimenting, and growing, and I want to be there to support you in ways that are meaningful to you." Spouses want to experience this deep soul connection, with understanding and patience, and without judgment. When do children need to feel loved, affirmed, and supported? All day every day, from birth into adulthood.

Sadly, when we encounter stress in our most important relationships, we usually default to high control—we try to control our emotions by pushing them down into the recesses of our hearts, we try to control others by demanding compliance, or we try to control our risk by withdrawing from meaningful interactions. One way or another, we desperately want to regain control. I've found that the primary reason people ratchet up the level of control over their spouse and kids is fear. We're afraid the ones we love will make cataclysmic, life-altering, terrible decisions, so we try desperately to keep that from happening. To keep them safe and to protect them from negative consequences, we step in to make their decisions for them. That's perfectly good and right when our children are two and are running toward the street, but as kids develop more autonomy, they increasingly need us to provide two essentials: unconditional love and measured guidance. One of the main problems in our culture today is that young adults haven't had the opportunities to struggle enough to develop resilience and problem-solving skills. Then, when they leave home for college or a career, they lack the ability to make good decisions—about their friends, bosses, professors, money, time, habits, and the future.

THE ROLE OF PARENTS

As children grow up, the role of parents morphs from protector to coach to facilitator. Some of us felt very comfortable when our kids were little and helpless. We could pour all our affection and energy into providing all they needed. Their fragility brought out the best in us. But as kids grow through the stages into adolescence, we need to increasingly turn over decision-making to them. Will they make mistakes? Certainly. Will they learn from their mistakes? Only if we don't under-react by not caring or over-react by condemning them or stepping in to prevent any consequences. When our kids become young adults, we step back a little more, becoming a facilitator who listens and encourages but gives little direct advice. But of course, some of us feel very uncomfortable when our kids are very young—they seem really out of control!—but we thrive in our roles as coaches and facilitators as our kids grow up. The lesson is to pay attention to the seasons in our kids' lives when we feel most comfortable and competent, lean into those times, and learn to play our crucial roles in the other seasons. In every relationship and at every stage, we follow the pattern of connecting, inspiring, building, and empowering those we love.

A couple brought their six-year-old son to see me. He was, they explained when he wasn't in the room, quite anxious around other children, so much so that he was unable to develop friendships and was afraid to attempt projects in school. They told me how completely they had been involved in every aspect of their son's life, and the problem instantly became clear. I explained the basic principle of strength-based parenting: It's not the parents' job to protect their kids from every painful consequence; it's to prepare them to experience life in its fullness. I explained, "You are very caring parents, but paradoxically, you're overly involved at the expense of your son." My comment caught them off guard—they had no idea they were a major part of the problem. I began to help them reframe their roles from protectors to guides so they could help their son navigate the inevitable bumps and bruises of life. I asked, "How did you respond to your son when he was learning to walk?"

"What do you mean?" the mom asked.

"What did you do when he fell down?"

"We picked him up so he could walk again."

"What would have happened if you'd waited so he could stand up again on his own?"

They looked perplexed, so I explained, "When we run to fix our children's problems, we make them dependent on us. But when we let them figure out a solution and act on it, they develop self-confidence and resilience." The parents' eyes widened. They were getting the picture, so I continued, "My guess is that you've treated him this way from then until now. You believed you were loving him well by protecting him, but you got in the way of him developing crucial life skills." I let this sink in for a few seconds, and then I told them, "I'm going to ask you to do something that's contrary to every instinct you've lived by. Let your son experience the natural consequences of his decisions. Some of them will hurt, but pain is a marvelous teacher. In fact, we learn some of life's most important lessons from the pain we experience. Then, when you see evidence of wisdom, strength, tenacity, and other important traits, affirm them. I assure you; it will feel very uncomfortable at first, but you'll see remarkable progress in your son. As you make these changes, you'll also see huge dividends in your relationship with him as he grows up. If you don't change, someday he'll resent you for dominating him, but if you gradually become a coach instead of a protector, he'll appreciate you."

The rest of the story is that change was incredibly difficult for the parents. Being consumed with their son's every decision and every circumstance had been deeply rooted in their neuroplasticity, and it took exceptional diligence to change their brain wiring. When they returned for the third appointment, they voiced their frustration with the process. I told them, "You're son is trying to get a need met, and you've taught him that you're more than willing to meet it without him needing to do anything. He has learned to be helpless. The need isn't wrong, but he has depended on you to meet it. Now you need to give him options: this or that, but neither of them is for you to jump in to fix it. If parents give kids one option, they easily say, 'no,' but if we give them a choice, they soon realize every decision has consequences, and they have the authority to choose the one they want. So, for instance, 'Johnny, you can sit and eat your supper or go to your room and do your homework.' We need to give children—even little children and especially older ones—the opportunity to choose an option and experience the consequences."

Three months after they initially came to see me, these parents and their son had turned a corner. The mom and dad had a very different perspective on "good parenting," and their son was thriving. Already, his confidence had grown, he had made a couple of friends, and his mood was completely different. "We see strengths in him we couldn't have imagined a few weeks ago," his mother marveled. "He's pleasant, more self-controlled. He knows that if he acts out, we're predictable—we aren't going to give him what he's asking for. We came up with a new slogan: 'Whatever you whine for, you automatically don't get.' We're seeing many more strengths, and we're talking about those instead of trying to control his complaining. You wouldn't believe how that has changed our relationships!"

Oh, but I would. I've seen it so many times that I expect family connections to radically change when parents see their roles more clearly. When kids want attention, some act out to yell, "I'm here! See me! Pay attention to me!" But others withdraw. They're whispering, "I'm here, but I hope you don't notice me. If I call attention to myself, I may be hurt worse than if I stay invisible." Both responses are ways children (and adults) try to cope with unmet needs. As we've seen throughout this book, people certainly need our attention, but to inspire, build, and empower them, not to smother them or fix problems they need to handle on their own.

All of us have had the experience of being in a grocery store and watching a child whine and scream for something she wants. Far too often, the parent is embarrassed and quickly gives in, which reinforces this demanding behavior. A better approach is to respond, "I can see it's time to go home." Leave the cart with an employee so all the items can be put back, take the child to the car, drive home, and explain, "You robbed me of my time shopping, so you're going to help me around the house. We're going to do a task together." It might be mopping the floor, raking leaves, or any of a hundred other chores. When kids act up, most parents put them in "time out." My approach is different: I want parents to "time in" with their kids by doing something purposeful together. When I used this strategy when my sons were young, they sometimes pouted and refused to help. If I was working in the yard, I put a chair in the grass and told them to sit there and watch me work. Within a few minutes, they got up and started helping me. They didn't like sitting alone. When children are out of control, it means they need us to connect with them—not to cave in and give them what they want, but to engage with them in an alternate, more productive way.

> ## Today, many parents function more like Uber drivers than parents.

The old saying is true: Parents need to give their kids both "roots and wings"—deep roots of affirmation, affection, and stability, and wide wings to soar, take wise risks, and see life as an adventure. If they haven't had enough opportunities to become wise through trial and error, they often make foolish decisions and replicate dysfunction when they grow up and have their families. Kids need to develop personal values, a deep sense of right and wrong, the value of ambiguity, gratitude for what they have, and integrity that comes from the heart. When kids develop these traits, they do the right thing even when no one is watching.

Today, many parents function more like Uber drivers than parents. Their kids are involved in sports, dance, theater, clubs, and other activities, so the only time they're together is running out the door and in the car. One outside activity is fine, but parents need to structure the week so there's plenty of time to be together. Many families create rituals, like pizza and game night, or dramatic readings, or something else that brings them together. We can't force deep, meaningful conversations with our children, especially adolescents, but we can be around them enough, and affirm them enough, so that rich conversations "just happen." A dad told me that his high school son was actively involved on the tennis team, and the team traveled at least once a week. "He was pretty preoccupied with school and tennis, but sometimes he knocked on our door after my wife and I had been asleep for an hour or so. That was when he wanted to talk, and I made sure I was available—mentally and emotionally—to be there with him." Some of the most powerful conversations we have with our children aren't because we want to impart a lesson, but when we're together doing something mundane like shopping, working in the yard, or watching a favorite show. When they feel respected (because we see them as valued people, not creatures to be contained), spontaneous and meaningful connections happen organically. Love and respect are the greatest gifts we can give our children.

STRATEGIES FOR STRENGTHS-BASED PARENTING

Unlike a traditional parenting approach that focuses on avoiding risk and correcting negative behaviors, strengths-based parenting focuses on relational interactions and capacity-building strategies that will strengthen a child's ability to flourish and meet life's challenges with thoughtfulness, confidence, purpose, and empathy. While the journey of each child is shaped by a range of factors from the society and culture they are raised in, there are some critical principles and ideas that influence and direct the strengths-based approach to raising competent and resilient children. Nine important strategies include:

1) See your child as "at potential," not "at risk."

The guiding mindset of strengths-based parents is that their children are amazing and need to understand their unique potential and its implications for their life's journey. It's not about being afraid for children and protecting them from all stress and potential risks, which often creates an enhanced vulnerability because they have not learned to successfully negotiate life's challenges. Rather, strengths-based parents believe in the ability of children to successfully overcome developmentally appropriate challenges, learn from them, and develop successful coping behaviors.

2) Prepare your child to walk the path.

The purpose of strengths-based parenting is to build the capacity of a child to flourish—an inside-out process, not an outside-in. The focus is on the *process* of development instead of some specific *outcome*. The principle is clear: Focus on the process and the behaviors will look after themselves. Competent and resilient children innately respond to challenges in constructive ways and slowly develop the essential strengths and character traits of successful and productive members of society.

3) Connect before teaching and directing.

The foundation of a secure, trusting, and loving parent-child relationship is essential for children to develop resilience. Children need to know they will always be cared for and supported in consistent ways so they feel safe, valued, competent, and confident about their future. Children who feel valued by their parents typically embrace the guidance being offered. A secure attachment to parents or caregivers early in life gives a child a solid foundation for developing trust, self-esteem, self-control, and confidence, which are essential building blocks for learning how to empower oneself and forming healthy relationships. It's about accepting each child for who he is, not what you want him to be. Healthy parent-child relationships facilitate the embrace of the parents' values so teenagers have clear, attractive choices during their formative adolescent years because they value the relationship and don't want to disappoint those they care about.

4) Help your child learn from mistakes.

Strengths-based parents understand that loving children isn't based on whether or not they make mistakes. We need to clearly communicate to our children that mistakes are not only accepted but expected. The focus of parenting is helping a child try new things, knowing that not every effort will result in success. But it's important to keep trying, understanding why it didn't work, and exploring better options—a pattern that promotes continued growth. Children need to know that making mistakes won't define who they are; rather, what they do with the mistakes will define them. Parents should serve as role models for dealing with mistakes and setbacks with calm and reflection. Your example teaches your child what it means to be human.

5) Focus more on what's right and why it's right.

Children learn best from parents who regularly reinforce appropriate behavior that a child engages in as opposed to continually challenging what's wrong. Parents need to celebrate a child's accomplishments and emphasize the steps of appropriate and successful coping behavior. It's important to support a child's unique strengths that lead to small successes and continue building on them toward more challenging opportunities—stretching your child to succeed more than they thought they could. This process leads to the development of a "growth mindset" that embraces challenges, persists in the face of setbacks, sees effort as an important key to success, learns from constructive criticism, welcomes good advice, and inspires others to be successful. Developing a child's strengths is a process based on developmentally appropriate, realistic expectations.

6) Understand the importance of re-writing negative scripts.

If your current parenting strategy isn't working, it's important to understand that the reason has more to do with us than our children. Strengths-based parenting sees change as a parent-driven process—if you want to see positive change in your children, you need to start with yourself. In our roles as a teacher (when our children are ages one to twelve) and facilitator (ages thirteen to eighteen), we often reflect beliefs that create a disconnect with our child, including:

- "One size fits all: all children can be parented the same way."
- "It's not my job to change. It's my child's role to just obey."
- "My child should be more appreciative of all my hard work and parental support."
- "My expectations and goals as a parent are realistic—if I say so."
- "This was the way I was parented—so it's good enough for you."

7) Choose your battles.

Parenting is full of battles—some are important to engage in and others aren't. If you try to fight every battle that comes your way, you'll burn out and frustrate your children. Neither is a good

outcome! Children who have overly controlling parents tend to choose one or several of the following strategies:
- They agree with you to your face, while doing whatever they want behind your back.
- They defy you, since they think that no matter what they do they can't make you happy.
- They wait for their freedom, then they'll do all that they can to prove you can't control them anymore.

The solution isn't to demand unquestioning compliance or to be overly controlling. Strengths-based parents understand the need to set boundaries in ways that are balanced and promote opportunities to build trust. Sometimes, letting go or getting out of the way is the wisest thing a parent can do.

8) Build resiliency through good communication.

Strengths-based parents understand that although a lot of time involves telling children what to do or stop doing (especially when they're very young), listening is just as important, if not more so. A child's confidence is rooted in the important people in their lives listening to them and understanding them. It's important to be ready to listen when children want to talk, to give them our full attention, to have regular conversations about what is going on in their daily lives, and to ask them for ideas and opinions in family discussions. We need to listen even when we disagree, be willing to talk about any subject, and provide comfort and assurance. Parents need to model good communication by speaking in a way that is respectful and acknowledges the strengths of the child.

9) Widen the circle to develop responsibility, compassion, and a social conscience.

Outside the immediate family, children need connections to multiple groups of friends, relatives, school staff, and community members. The more supportive and positive their connections, the more children feel a sense of belonging to a larger community that values them as contributing members. In helping others, children realize that others have needs, and they can contribute to the solution as part of a safe and supportive community. If parents support their children by connecting to organizations that reinforce the values they cherish, children learn that others expect them to play fair, be honest and loyal, and be responsible and compassionate. It takes a village to raise a child, and parents need to purposefully invite the right people into their children's lives.

Children require hope and the courage to follow their goals. These qualities help them develop the inner strengths and character traits necessary to succeed despite the many challenges they inevitably face. To develop a thriving mindset, children need more than just support and care. They need daily affirmation and encouragement, parents' active involvement in their lives, opportunities to participate in the community, and a supportive neighborhood. Children require boundaries, values, realistic expectations, and caring schools. While there is no precise formula, there are common themes and opportunities that all parents must provide to their children—placing the emphasis of parenting on what it takes to raise resilient children.

BENCHMARKS

Take a mental inventory of your communication with your child over the past week, and ask yourself the following questions:

- Do my messages convey and teach respect?
- Am I putting the relationship before directing?
- Am I fostering realistic expectations?
- Am I helping my child to problem solve?
- Am I teaching empathy and compassion?
- Am I promoting self-discipline and control?
- Am I setting limits in ways that permit learning as opposed to resentment?
- Am I validating what my child says?
- Do my children know that I value their input?
- Do my children know how special they are to me?
- Do my children know that mistakes are part of the process of learning?
- Am I comfortable acknowledging my own mistakes and apologizing to my child?

Self-reflection is essential if we want our relationships with our children to flourish. Honesty—with ourselves and with those who care about us—is the first step of growth and change. We can then acquire new, positive strategies, adapt to challenges, take risks, learn from our mistakes, and stay on the path to the great adventure of having meaningful connections with our growing children.

IN MARRIAGE

When couples come for counseling, probably 90 percent of them are asking for help with at least one of four common marital issues: money, sex, kids, and in-laws. Most couples began their engagement with stars in their eyes and high hopes for authentic love for the rest of their lives together, but somewhere along the road, the stress of life and the weight of unresolved hurts have caused their relationship to be something far less than what they dreamed it would be. It's helpful to see these relationships on a broad continuum:

- Some couples walk into a counseling office with genuine contempt for each other. They've lived in an armed truce for years, blaming one another for any and every perceived fault. They're not sure they have any hope for a future.
- Some barely tolerate each other. By this point, past hurts have accumulated. They know what topics are off-limits, so they avoid them as much as possible. They exist in the same home, but they live with high walls to protect themselves from being hurt again.
- Some are caring friends who get along well, but they don't feel fully known and loved. Many "nice" couples fit into this category.
- And some couples have progressed from infatuation when they first married through the friction of learning the fine

art of true affection. They know love isn't just a pleasant feeling. They are tenacious about protecting and advancing their relationship. No topic is off-limits. They're willing and able to be vulnerable because they trust the other will handle them with tenderness and respect.

When a husband and wife come because they've hit a wall in their relationship and they believe their marriage can be so much more than being roommates, I ask each of them, "What would it look like to be in love with each other? What does genuine affection feel like? What would your spouse need to do for you to feel that way?" If there's even an ounce of hope, most couples are more than willing to enter into this conversation. We then explore what progress toward real love will look like. Quite often, one or both of them have unhealed wounds, perhaps from hurts that happened many years ago and have never been resolved.

We talk about what they each liked about the other when they were dating and first married. These memories usually trigger hopeful feelings, and we talk about those seasons when love was palpable. We then discuss what it might mean for those feelings to be brought into the present. What would need to change? What would be the payoffs for each of them?

I ask each one, "What would it look like for your spouse to be attentive to your needs?" Almost invariably, they share stories about times when they felt known, pursued, understood, and adored—times when words weren't just words but were heartwarming bonds of commitment. As usual, the solution is found in the story.

Change comes from acting, and feelings will follow.

Each one may have walked into the room under the assumption that it's 99 percent the other person's fault, so I make sure they know progress is a shared responsibility: both need to be honest, both need to listen, and both need to affirm the other. Often people are defiant and insist, "I'll act more loving when I feel more loved."

I respond, "Then you won't get very far. In fact, you'll stay stuck where you've been. Change comes from acting, and feelings will follow. In other words, if people act in ways that make the other person feel loved, the actions will generate the emotion of love . . . in both of you."

So, one side of the solution is for each one to act in ways that demonstrate a deeper, more authentic affection, but the other side is the response. I ask, "If he (or she) acts in the way you say will communicate love, how will you respond?" It's not a superficial question. Many couples get blocked at this crucial point because the other person doesn't show enough appreciation, or more often, the recipient doesn't trust that the gestures are genuine, so the ice doesn't melt. If your spouse attempts to move forward, it's important to give positive feedback. No, he (or she) may not have said it or done it perfectly, but we applaud progress, not perfection.

An exercise that adds an interesting twist is when I tell couples, "Apply the principles of active love on Tuesday, Thursday, and

Saturday, and on Sunday, talk about what was different on those days." The responses are fascinating. Often people tell me, "I felt a lot closer to him (or her) on those three days, but the other days were terrible . . . so I guess taking the initiative to love each other really works!"

Different lived experiences can create distance or delight—it depends on your point of view. My wife and I come from very different backgrounds, so we have divergent opinions about many topics. If we didn't love and respect each other, these differences could drive a wedge between us, but with love and respect, we learn from each other . . . and even amaze each other. I understand that our backgrounds can cause friction. When she responds to a situation or a comment that makes me feel uncomfortable, I've learned that she's acting out of her lived experience, so I don't take it personally. And heaven knows, she's had to learn that I act out of my past experiences, too! If she's frustrated with me, I don't bark, "Why are you always so angry at me?" It doesn't take a PhD in psychology to anticipate the kind of response this remark will elicit. Instead, I invite her to join me in exploring her past: "I can tell there's something here that's making you feel uncomfortable. I'd like to talk about that. I don't want to frustrate you. I want to know where that's coming from so I can treat you in a way that makes you feel safe and loved."

We can take the principles and perspectives of a flourishing life into our most important relationships. The people who live under our roofs are in our inner circle . . . or they should be . . . and they can be. They matter to us, and we matter to them. The applications of flourishing are the same wherever we go. We need to make sure we know them and live them so we have a positive impact on those who know us best.

Think about it:
1) How would you describe the changing role of parents as kids grow from infancy to childhood to adolescence to become young adults?
2) At which stage of your children's development do (or did) you feel most comfortable? Which one feels most uncomfortable? Explain your answer.
3) If you have children or grandchildren, what are some concrete ways you can connect with, inspire, build, and empower each of them?
4) Look back at the strategies of strengths-based parenting. Which of the nine are you doing well? Which one(s) needs improvement?
5) On the continuum from contempt to tolerating to caring to genuine love, what are the challenges and payoffs of moving toward a flourishing marriage?
6) If you're married, are you willing to ask your spouse, "What would it look like for me to be attentive to your needs?" When and how will you enter this conversation and ask the question of your spouse?
7) What are some reasons it's important to understand that present marital frustrations are rooted in past lived experiences?

CHAPTER 11

Flourishing at Work

Flourishing at work isn't just about achieving professional success; it's about finding purpose, meaning, and fulfillment in your daily tasks, creating a sense of fulfillment that extends beyond the workplace.
—Unknown

A Gallup survey of people at work focused on employee engagement, measured by the level of involvement and enthusiasm. The study found that only 23 percent of employees across the globe and 32 percent in America are truly engaged in their work. This means that the vast majority of people at work today aren't engaged or are actively disengaged, even though their supervisors have tried to help them connect with the vision of the companies. The authors of the research explain:

> *One of the most common mistakes companies make is to approach engagement as a sporadic exercise in making their employees feel happy—usually around the time when a survey is coming up.*
>
> *It's true that we describe engaged employees as "enthusiastic." And surveys play a big role in measuring staff engagement. But it's not that simple.*
>
> *Employees need more than a fleeting warm-fuzzy feeling and a good paycheck (even if it helps them respond positively on a survey) to invest in their work and achieve more for your company.*
>
> *People want purpose and meaning from their work. They want to be known for what makes them unique. This is what drives employee engagement.*
>
> *And they want relationships, particularly with a manager who can coach them to the next level. This is who drives employee engagement.*
>
> *One of Gallup's biggest discoveries: the manager or team leader alone counts for 70 percent of the variance in team engagement.*[29]

My observations of people and their careers are consistent with Gallup's conclusions—people need work that corresponds to their purpose and passion. Quite often, a person's "bent" is noticeable at an early age. For instance, an unusually caring child may eventually choose a career as a veterinarian, nurse,

---

29 "What Is Employee Engagement and How Do You Improve It?" *Gallup*, https://www.gallup.com/workplace/285674/improve-employee-engagement-workplace.aspx.

or therapist, and a child who shows an aptitude for building blocks and structures may become an architect, engineer, or builder. Their inner spirit is searching for a role where it can be expressed to its fullest.

Searching. That's a key factor for each of us as we consider where we'll invest our time and talents. Those who take the first job offered to them often become frustrated when the responsibilities don't challenge and inspire them beyond making a decent living. A few years ago, I met with an executive at an oil company who told me that he had been interviewing recent engineering graduates. One young man used the interview to ask some pointed questions: "I want to know more about your company. What are your values?" "How do you see your company's impact on the environment?" "What is your role in community partnerships?" The executive realized this candidate wanted to know if the company had a purpose beyond maximizing the share price for investors. He wanted to see if his purpose and passion aligned with the executive's and the company's. The executive hired the young man on the spot.

> **There's never a bad time to identify or refine our purpose and values.**

In finding the right career, the first step is to clarify our purpose and values. Instead of just absorbing the culture of a company by osmosis, it's far healthier to spend time looking at our stories to see what has mattered to us, what has inspired us, and what we've done well that has given us satisfaction. It's helpful to think through this analysis when we're young, but there's never a bad time to identify or refine our purpose and values. Today, I'm at the age when many people retire, but I'm not looking forward to something better. What I do every day *is* better! I get up every day with a sense of adventure: Will someone cross my path today who needs to be connected, inspired, built, and empowered? Unless I stay in a closet all day, the answer is always, "Yes!" I like being around people, and I'm thrilled when I see lightbulbs of insight turn on. I'm amazed that God could use me to inspire people to flourish. That never gets old.

Hard work may be the cornerstone of the Puritan work ethic, but that cornerstone must be grounded in something meaningful. Hard work is worthwhile if we learn and grow from the experience, it develops our character, advances who we want to become, and it has a powerful and positive impact on others.

The Gallup survey identifies four levels of employee engagement:

- At the most fundamental level, employees are asking, "What do I get out of working here?" The answers are generally about salary, benefits, and a low amount of stress.

- The second level changes the focus to, "What do I give?" This is about individual contribution, job fit, appreciation for work, and personal accomplishment.
- The third level is about relationships: "Do I belong?" When people feel known and heard, trust becomes the foundation of strong relationships. Together, the team accomplishes more than the sum of individual efforts.
- The fourth level is about the future: "How do I grow?" In a supportive, collaborative environment employees feel inspired, not threatened, by challenges. They put themselves in a position to learn new lessons, sharpen existing skills, and acquire new ones.[30]

It's certainly possible that people on a team may be at different levels—some are just getting their feet wet in launching their careers, some are in the early stages of identifying what they do with excellence, and others have developed stability in their relationships so they feel free to be creative.

The alignment of our purpose with the purpose of the company is important at every level of corporate life, from the custodian to the CEO. No job is just a job. The people at the lowest level of the organizational chart need a strengths-based approach to their work just as much as those in the C-suite. Every role is crucial so that teams function, people thrive, and customers and clients are served with excellence. When President Kennedy toured NASA in 1962, he noticed a janitor carrying a broom. He

---

30 "What Is Employee Engagement?", *Gallup*.

stopped, walked over to the man, and said, "Hi, I'm Jack Kennedy. What are you doing?"

The janitor didn't miss a beat. He responded, "Well, Mr. President, I'm helping put a man on the moon." This man went to work each day with the conviction that his contribution mattered. With each sweep of his broom, he was making history.

In an article in *Inc.,* Dave Kerpen, founder and CEO of Apprentice, writes that "purpose-driven" companies thrive for five reasons:

1) Purpose inspires your team.

   In my experience, nothing motivates a team more than knowing they're working toward a meaningful goal. It's not just about clocking in and out; *it's about contributing to a larger mission. When employees believe in the purpose of their organization, they become more engaged, more productive, and more likely to stay with the company.*

2) Purpose attracts and retains customers.

   "Purpose differentiates you by tapping into the hearts and minds of customers who are looking for more than just products or services. This leads to increased loyalty and customer retention."

3) Purpose differentiates you in the market.

   "Purpose gives you a unique identity, a compelling story to tell, and a genuine connection with your audience. It's a powerful differentiator that can absolutely give you a competitive edge."

4) Purpose drives innovation.

   When we're motivated by a deeper meaning and a desire to make a positive impact, we're driven to think differently, explore new possibilities, and challenge the status quo. Purpose creates a fertile ground for creativity, encouraging us to ask the right questions and seek more innovative solutions to the problems we face.

5) Purpose is good for the bottom line.

   When a company embraces a strong sense of purpose, it becomes more than just a profit-making machine. It becomes a force for positive change in the world. And guess what? Customers, employees, and investors are all taking notice. They're gravitating toward purpose-driven brands because they too want to be a part of something meaningful.

Purpose, Kerpen concludes, "is the compass that guides us, the motivation that drives us, and the essence that defines us. As we look to the future, let's not chase money, scale or success—let's chase purpose."[31]

A "GOOD ENOUGH" FIT

For me, there's no dichotomy between my personal life and my career. I have the same purpose wherever I go. I treat my family and those I consult with and counsel in the same way—with

---

[31] Dave Kerpen, "5 Reasons to Embrace a Purpose-Driven Approach in Business," *Inc.*, https://www.inc.com/dave-kerpen/5-reasons-to-embrace-a-purpose-driven-approach-in-business.html

honor, respect, and admiration. My purpose and values are consistent in every conversation and every task.

> No job is a perfect fit. All work includes some drudgery, but it shouldn't be all drudgery.

But purpose and values aren't static; they evolve as we grow in wisdom, we have more varied experiences, and we receive feedback from people we trust. My purpose as an eighteen-year-old was much less defined than when I was forty . . . or fifty . . . or sixty. As we work in a current role, our competence increases, and we may find that we're quite skilled at something we've never tried before. At the same time, we develop soft skills in interpersonal relationships, and we're more adept at leading people, bringing out the best in them, and handling conflict with a blend of truth and grace.

No job is a perfect fit. All work includes *some* drudgery, but it should include aspects of meaningfulness, alignment with our strengths, and reflect our evolving sense of purpose in our lives. I love my work, but some days it's exhausting, and I want to find an escape hatch. A "good enough fit" gives us opportunities to be creative, sharpen our skills, collaborate with others, and see the impact of our work on the lives of others. We usually find ourselves in a job that has many qualities that align with our purpose but some that don't. The question is always: How close is good enough? If we enjoy working with the people around us and we have a genuine sense of accomplishment, we can put up with some rough edges. If, however, the negatives are too significant, and our attempts to resolve them have proven unproductive (or counterproductive), it may be time to look for a better fit.

A young woman proved to be an excellent, rising leader in a marketing firm, and she received an offer to become a partner in a larger company. The salary increase was nice, but she was especially interested in two things: the quality of the team she would lead and the scope of opportunities to have an impact. For the first six months at her new job, she excelled. She felt fulfilled and validated, and she loved working with her team. But something in the CEO flipped at about that time. In a matter of weeks, she became the object of his ridicule. She tried to talk to him to determine the cause of his sudden disapproval, but he brushed her off and claimed, "Oh, it's nothing. I was just having a bad day. Forget it." But it wasn't just a bad day. It was a bad week, a bad month, and soon a bad quarter. She wondered how she'd missed any signs that the CEO was mercurial, but a trusted friend in the company explained, "I think he feels threatened by your skills and confidence." That insight was only marginally helpful. She still had to find ways to cope with his disapproval, which not only became a dark cloud over her but over her team because they were guilty by association. She found a professional coach to help her wade through the confusion and chart a path forward. For months, she tried to address the issue, but there was no progress. Finally, she left the company and started her own firm. She recalls:

> *It was, as Dickens said, "the best of times, it was the worst of times." I loved the people I worked with, and the job perfectly fit my talents. I stayed as long as I could, but it was killing me—I wasn't sleeping, I lost weight, I was grouchy at home. Many of the people at the company are still good friends. They weren't the brunt of the attacks, so they felt okay about staying, but it was time for me to go. I learned a lot from the experience. By enduring as long as I did, I gained confidence in my insights, my ability to lead, and my dedication to create a supportive culture. I wouldn't go back there, but I took a lot from the experience.*

Did you notice the elements of a flourishing life in her story? She connected strongly with the people on her team, and in the midst of personal attacks, they supported each other. Her coach inspired her to trust her perceptions instead of absorbing unwarranted blame, and with renewed confidence, she inspired the people on her team. Together, they built their skills, refined their approach to clients, and created an effective structure to serve people inside and outside the company. When she felt confused and powerless, her coach infused her with a renewed vision that she could make good decisions and relate to her CEO without reacting. She felt empowered to start her marketing firm, and today, she's thriving.

KEY QUESTIONS

If you're one of those people who is actively engaged and fulfilled in your career, take some time to answer these questions:

- As you look back at your childhood and when you were a young adult, what were the signs that this might be a good career fit for you?
- What about your current job fits really well? . . . fairly well? . . . not so well?
- In what ways are your purposes at home and at work consistent?
- How are you actively and purposefully helping others flourish? How well are you connecting, inspiring, building, and empowering?

If you're passively disengaged—your body is at work, but your mind and heart are often somewhere else—answer these questions:

- When you were young, what activities did you enjoy? What did adults affirm that you did well?
- Has there been a time when you had a clear sense of purpose? If so, describe that season of your life.
- Specifically, what about your current role is less than inspiring?

- If you had a powerful purpose, would you stay at that job and make it work well for you, or would you look for a better fit?

If you're actively disengaged—that is, resistant to your supervisor and a pain to the people who are trying to do a good job—answer these questions:

- Look back at the time when you were a child through when you were a young adult. What activities did you enjoy? What did adults affirm that you did well?
- Defiance is a way to make sense of the past. It says, "I'm not going to take it anymore!" Does that statement hit home for you? Why or why not?
- What would it look like for you to enter the process of connecting with a wise, supportive person, letting your heart be inspired to something far better than today, building your skills and insights, and being empowered to be your best?
- Are you willing to do what it takes to flourish? Explain your answer.

Take your time answering these questions. There are no bonus points for speed! It's often helpful to discuss your answers with someone you trust, someone who can challenge your negative assumptions and encourage you to reach higher. Don't settle for being passively engaged or actively disengaged in your work. Do something about it!

Think about it:
1) Are you surprised at the Gallup survey report that the vast majority of people are passively engaged or actively disengaged at work? Explain your answer.
2) How would you state and explain the significance of your purpose in life?
3) Review the Key Questions and answer the ones that fit your attitude at work today.

CHAPTER 12

Unleash Your Potential!

Challenges are what make life interesting and overcoming them is what makes life meaningful.
—quoted by Joshua Marine

I met Danny Lawson when he played for the Calgary Flames, and we became close friends. Danny grew up in an impoverished home, but he had dreams of using his hockey talents as a ticket to something far better. He started his career in the Canadian junior league for the Hamilton Red Wings. In '67-'68, he finished second in scoring and was named an All Star.

He then played for the Detroit Red Wings in the NHL, and when a rival league opened in 1972, Danny accepted an offer from the Philadelphia Blazers. He played on the same team as the superstar

Bobby Hull, but at the end of the season, Danny had more goals than the legend. He was named to the league's First Team All Stars.

For the next several years, Danny bounced from one team to another. By 1977, his playing days were over, and he retired from the game as a player for the Flames. That's where I come into the story.

I was, of course, intrigued by the career of a star athlete, but as we got to know each other, I saw another side of Danny. He had devoted his life to being the very best hockey player he could be, and he had excelled, but when he hung up his skates, he no longer knew who he was. . . . he struggled to find any sense of purpose beyond the rink. He shared his emotional distress with me, and it was obvious he needed someone to connect with him more profoundly than those who were running into him on the ice. My wife and I invited him to live with us, and he was part of our family for four years.

About three years into Danny's time with us, he developed throat cancer. The oncologist outlined a treatment plan of surgery that would, the doctor predicted, give Danny many more years. But the surgery would cause his face to be a bit disfigured. I was sure that was a minor obstacle, but I soon discovered it was much more than that to Danny. He told the doctor that he refused the surgery because he wanted his legacy of a healthy athlete more than he wanted fifteen to twenty more years of life.

The cancer spread quickly, and only months later, I sat at Danny's bedside as he slipped away. I was grieved to lose a friend, and I was deeply saddened that he had valued his physical appearance over life itself. He wanted people to remember him as the handsome star athlete on the posters, and he was willing to pay the highest price for that legacy.

Danny's story illustrates a warning for each of us: If we live in the past, we'll struggle in the present, and we'll have no future. Many people live in a painful past—the wounds and betrayals at the hands of people they trusted haunt them all day every day. In spare moments, their daydreams and nightmares go back to those events. They relive the excruciating hurts, and they relive thoughts of getting even. But others, like Danny, live in past glories. Their success has become an anvil weighing them down instead of a stepping stone to something even better.

Now that we are nearing the end of the book, let me remind you: All of us have amazing potential for growth, success, and impact . . . but only if we learn to focus on our strengths instead of our flaws and failures.

Over the years, I've met with people from a vast array of backgrounds—from those who have been stunningly successful to those who had lost any vestige of hope for a better life. It may be surprising (though at this point in your reading, it probably isn't) that some of those who enjoy the trappings of financial and professional success are miserable because their success has come at the expense of strained and broken relationships. The point is that social status, wealth, and fame can be poor substitutes for a life of genuine flourishing. Thankfully, I've known some of these "rich and famous" who are living authentic flourishing lives, with strong connections, a compelling sense of purpose, ordered priorities, and enough self-care so they can be at their best for every person and in each situation. But to be honest, I'm more thrilled and amazed when I meet people like Bethany (see her story in the first chapter), whose lives seemed to be dead ends, but with support, encouragement, and tenacity, are now thriving.

An open door to a flourishing life is in front of all of us . . . even you.

> Their success has become an anvil weighing them down instead of a stepping stone to something even better.

In this book, we've seen the tremendous benefits of focusing on strengths—ours and others'—instead of flaws, weaknesses, and failures. One outlook produces confidence and creativity; the other discourages us or drives us to prove ourselves . . . or both. We need to be around people who see us as inherently valuable, people who connect deeply with us, who see the spark of potential in us, help us build and expand our skills, and empower us to excel more than we ever dreamed possible. Do you have people like that in your life?

Flourishing begins with us, but it doesn't end with us. We're vessels that spill out what's inside us—especially when we're shaken! It is a dictum of life that our self-perception determines how we treat others. If we believe we're not valuable, we may see others as nuisances or stepping stones to our own success; if we feel unloved (and worse, unlovable), we'll have great difficulty expressing genuine love for others; if we focus on our "bad luck" and what's gone so wrong so long for us, we probably won't inspire too many people—especially those close to us.

In this chapter, I want to draw all the concepts of the book together into a road map for your future. A number of researchers have introduced the idea that the most effective way to enhance our capacity to thrive during challenging times is to train our brains to be more resilient and competent by using our stressors to our advantage.[32] Strategies to build your capacity to flourish and experience positive well-being include:

1) Cultivate a strengths-based perspective.

    At every moment of every day, we have a choice: to focus on what's wrong with us or what's right with us. It matters ... it matters a lot! Yes, we all have weaknesses, past failures, and things we'd rather forget, but we also have strengths, successes, and memories that can inspire us to greater heights.

---

32 Bonnie Benard and Sara Truebridge,"A shift in thinking: Influencing social worker's beliefs about individual and family resilience to enhance well-being and success for all," In *The Strengths Perspective in Social Work*, ed. D. Saleebey (Oxford University Press, 2013).
Dweck, C. S. (2006). *Mindset: The new psychology of success.* Random House.
Seligman, M. (2011). *Flourish.* London: Nicholas Brealey Publishing.
Southwick, S. M., & amp; Charney, D. S. (2012). *Resilience: The science of mastering life's greatest challenges.* New York, NY, US: Cambridge University Press.

A flaws-based perspective produces worry, fretting, anger, revenge, and sadness. Negative, painful conclusions about ourselves consume our minds and prevent us from finding comfort and hope. Instead, focus your attention on possibilities, passions, gratitude, compassion, and growth.

2) Nurture your sense of empowerment.

Your willingness to take action in difficult and stressful situations is enhanced when you have confidence in your own capabilities, knowledge of your strengths, and the belief that you can use challenges to learn, grow, and develop. Our confidence and sense of empowerment increase as new challenges are creatively engaged and resolved with strengths-focused strategies.

3) Reframe your stressful experiences.

Although we can't change our past experiences, we can change how we understand and respond to them. They aren't the end of the world; they're the unexpected door to new possibilities. Those who feel distressed are desperate to simply survive, but those who learn to use those events in productive ways genuinely thrive.

4) Know who you need in your inner circle.

We need to build strong connections with others and reach out to them when we need help. It's tough to evaluate ourselves, so we need connections with people who are willing to provide honest feedback. When you have the right relationships, you can go well beyond the normal limits of your own energy and resolve issues that may seem impossible for one person to handle. To flourish we need to be willing to listen to others, learn from them, and take advice.

5) Be clear about your priorities.

Most crisis situations are filled with confusion and ambiguity. You'll be most effective if you can quickly decide what's most important and tune out distractions. This allows you to conserve your energy and achieve the best outcomes.

6) Be creative.

When you encounter an unexpected challenge, you need to determine how to address it. If you can stretch your brain to come up with a wide range of options that include new, unusual, or unexpected strategies, you have a better chance of a positive outcome. As a bonus, this strategy helps you see humor even in dark times.

7) Step out of your comfort zone.

In my years of research, I haven't discovered a personality profile of "natural flourishers"; instead, I've found people who don't settle for the status quo. They find out what they need to know and what they need to do, and they work hard to acquire the knowledge and skills necessary to get them where they want to go.

8) Follow your moral compass.

Our guiding principles and spiritual beliefs help us thrive during stressful and challenging times. The answer to a problem isn't always clear, but a step of faith based on our desire to value the potential in ourselves and others will always bear fruit.

9) Prioritize your well-being.

Self-care is an important part of staying physically, spiritually, and mentally healthy. For many of us, learning to take care of ourselves is a challenge. For whatever reason, we're often taught that it is a virtue to put the needs of our work, families, and other people ahead of our own needs. But it's okay to focus on yourself. In fact, it's the only way you're going to have the wisdom and strength to look after other people. Self-care will make you healthier, happier, and wiser.

10) Create meaning in your personal and professional role.

All of us play important roles of leading, caring, and serving. To thrive, we need to find meaning in what we do each day. A sense of purpose isn't an add-on; it's essential for a flourishing life. Ralph Waldo Emerson reportedly observed, "The purpose of life is not to be happy. It is to be useful, to be honorable, to be compassionate, to have it make some difference that you have lived and lived well."

Flourishing begins with us, but it doesn't end with us.

UNLEASH YOUR POTENTIAL! 215

Let me conclude with a quote from Dr. Mahesh Jethmalani that has become a time-proven formula for flourishing:

If you change your thoughts...
you will change your beliefs.
If you change your beliefs...
You will change your expectations.
If you change your expectations...
you will change your attitude.
If you change your attitude...
you will change your behavior.
If you change your behavior...
you will change your performance.
If you change your performance...
you will change your life.

Appendix

FLOURISHING FRAMEWORK STRENGTH DESCRIPTIONS

SELF-AWARENESS: A conscious understanding of one's own character, strengths, feelings, motives, and desires.

- Self-Esteem/Optimistic: Positive feelings of self-respect and hopefulness about the future.
- Strengths-Based Perspective/Confidence: Positive belief in one's capacity, strengths and ability to create success.
- Sense of Purpose/Direction: Knows what is important and holds clear values that guide their thoughts and actions.

SOCIAL-AWARENESS: The ability to understand social and ethical norms, take the perspective of and empathize with others, including those from diverse backgrounds and cultures.

- Empathic/Caring: Considerate of the needs of others and has insight into the feelings and circumstances from their point of view.

- Positive Social Skills: Can effectively communicate and interact with others in respectful ways.
- Social Conscience/Altruism: Believes that everyone should be treated equally and fairly.

SELF-MANAGEMENT: The ability to regulate one's emotions, thoughts, and behaviors effectively in different situations.

- Emotional Awareness/Self-Regulation: Can identify and clearly express feelings in constructive and self-regulated ways.
- Self-Efficacy/Empowered: A belief in one's ability to make choices and create positive change.
- Cognitive Flexibility/Adaptable: The mental ability to embrace alternative options as possible solutions.

SELF-CARE: "The ability to promote health, sense of purpose, prevent disease, maintain positive well-being even when faced with life challenges.

- Self-Kindness/Compassion: Ability to demonstrate warmth and understanding towards oneself.
- Spiritual Eagerness: Engaged in exploring one's spiritual sense of self and purpose in life.
- Health Aware/Active: An awareness of the benefits of daily exercise and proper nutrition.

HOME LIFE INFLUENCE/SUPPORT: A personal context where one experiences genuine and supportive relationships that exhibit care, supportive expectations and effective communication.

- Connectedness – Valued/Safe/Belonging: Positive relational support with a caregiver and feels valued and accepted.
- Positive Expectations/Supportive: Caregiver is a positive role model with supportive expectations.
- Positive Communication/Respect: Feels respected and safe to express feelings and concerns.

WORK/ROLE INFLUENCE/SUPPORT: A work/role context where one experiences genuine and supportive relationships that exhibit care, supportive expectations and effective communication.

- Connectedness – Valued/Safe/Belonging: Feels accepted, valued and an important member of the work/role culture.
- Positive Expectations/Support: Professional colleagues are encouraging and supportive developing meaningful goals.
- Positive Communication/Respect: Encouraged to share feelings knowing that they will be respectfully supported.

PEER INFLUENCE/SUPPORT: An interactive peer context where one experiences genuine and supportive relationships that exhibit acceptance, respectful support and affirmation of positive values.

- Positive Friends/Acceptance: Can initiate, develop and sustain positive/respectful peer friendships.
- Shared Values/Peer Refusal: Has a positive network of friends that are value driven in their efforts and aspirations.

LEARNING INFLUENCE/SUPPORT: A learning context where one's confidence to learn is nurtured by providing the support resources, scaffolding success and encouraging performance competence.

- Achievement Motivated: Has a strong work ethic and desire to be successful at school.
- Competence Focused: Strong learning capacity and ability to create innovative successes.
- Confidence Building: Feels confident to engage in and successfully complete academic tasks.

COMMUNITY INFLUENCE/SUPPORT: A community context where one experiences genuine and supportive relationships that exhibit care, supportive expectations and effective communication.

- Connectedness—Valued/Safe/Belonging: Connected to caring community adults and feels valued and encouraged.
- Positive Expectations/Supportive: Community is very supportive and realistic in their expectations of youth.
- Positive Communication/Involvement: Community values and encourages youth to be connected and share their feelings and concerns.

INTERNAL SOFT SKILLS/TRAITS: Personal traits and interpersonal strengths that supports one's capacity to interact with oneself.

- Perseverance/Grit: Stays focused on a task even in light of challenges or previous failures.
- Managing Stress/Mindfulness: Can cope with stressful situations by relaxing and being self-aware.
- Perceptiveness/Prudence: Is insightful and open to considering others points of view.
- Growth Mindset: Believes one's strengths and abilities can improve through hard work.
- Criticism/Change Receptive: Receptive to constructive advice and/or need to change.
- Integrity/Ethical/Courage: Has strong values and does what is right no matter the cost.

EXTERNAL SOFT SKILLS/TRAITS: Personal traits and intrapersonal strengths that support one's capacity to interact with and manage relationships with others.

- Communication/Listening: Able to clearly express thoughts and listen to understand.
- Empowering/Generous: Supports the success of others and puts their needs ahead of their own.
- Positive Interpersonal Skills: Capacity to initiate and maintain positive rapport in respectful ways.
- Diverse/Cultural Receptive: Respects and is receptive to the diverse beliefs of others.
- Managing Conflict/Expectations: The ability to negotiate differences and address unrealistic expectations.

- Collaborative/Team Player: Is a positive influence and likes to be part of collaborative activities.

MASTERY SKILLS/TRAITS: Personal traits and interpersonal strengths that support one's capacity to grow their potential, embrace the unknown and navigate new challenges in effective ways.

- Innovative/Creative: Is very creative and likes to think outside the box to create success.
- Knowledgeable/Intuitive: Has insight to life situations and how to respond to what is important.
- Critical Thinker/Problem Solver: Independent thinker who can explore options to solve problems.
- Good Judgement/Accountable: Reflects common sense and accepts responsibility for their decisions.
- Curious/Inquiry Skills: Presents as curious and will ask questions to find workable solutions.
- Continuous/Deep Learner: Eager to learn and presents as passionate about certain areas of interest.

www.ingramcontent.com/pod-product-compliance
Lightning Source LLC
Chambersburg PA
CBHW070533090426
42735CB00013B/2970